THE
ULTIMATE
CV

THE
ULTIMATE
CV THIRD EDITION

Win senior managerial positions with an outstanding resumé

Rachel Bishop-Firth

howto**books**

Published by How To Books Ltd,
3 Newtec Place, Magdalen Road,
Oxford OX4 1RE. United Kingdom.
Tel: (01865) 793806. Fax: (01865) 248780.
email: info@howtobooks.co.uk
http://www.howtobooks.co.uk

First edition 2000
Reprinted 2000
Second edition 2004
Third edition 2006

British Library Cataloguing in Publication Data
A catalogue record for this book is available from the British Library

ISBN-10: 1-84528-113-6
ISBN-13: 978-1-84528-113-7

Produced for How To Books by Deer Park Productions, Tavistock
Cover design by Baseline Arts Ltd, Oxford
Typeset by PDQ Typesetting, Newcastle-under-Lyme, Staffs.
Printed and bound by Cromwell Press, Trowbridge, Wiltshire

NOTE: The material contained in this book is set out in good faith for general guidance and no liability
can be accepted for loss or expense incurred as a result of relying in particular circumstances on
statements made in the book. The laws and regulations are complex and liable to change, and readers
should check the current position with the relevant authorities before making personal arrangements.

Contents

List of Illustrations

Preface

Competition in the job market for senior and professional roles is increasingly fierce, and your CV is a vital tool in winning the post that you want. Most job advertisements attract many more applicants than could possibly be interviewed. If your CV stands out from the rest – if the recruiter can see at a glance that you have just what their company needs – your chances of getting an interview are very much higher.

A successful CV is one that shows your experience, abilities and qualifications in the best possible light. This book will take you through the process of finding the approach that works for you. It covers:

- selecting an effective job hunting strategy
- identifying your personal key selling points
- grabbing the recruiter's attention to make them read your CV
- choosing an appropriate format and style for your CV
- selling yourself to the employer
- projecting a suitable professional image
- creating a winning covering letter
- preparing for your interview.

Most job hunters today send their CVs electronically and increasing numbers of organisations receive all their CVs this way. This new edition looks at the effect that this will have on one way that you write and send your CV.

I would like to dedicate this book to Andy.

With best wishes in your search for a new post,

Rachel Bishop-Firth

A Strategy for Success

Many job hunters try to maximise their chances of success simply by approaching as many employers as possible with a standard CV and covering letter. While this can work, it is usually too haphazard an approach for people at a managerial and professional level. If your career is important to you, you need to choose a role and company in which you can flourish – and you will usually have limited time in which to do this. You are therefore most likely to be successful if you:

- set your **goals**
- decide on a **strategy** to reach them
- **focus** on the best opportunities.

SETTING YOUR GOALS

Setting clear goals is a vital first step in your job search. You may already know exactly what you are looking for – if not, invest some time in deciding what you really want. The obvious basics are:

- type of work
- responsibilities
- development opportunities
- location
- minimum salary and benefits
- organisational culture.

There may be other points that are important for you. For example, you may want to work for a company that will pay for your MBA; you may want exposure to international business, or you may feel strongly about the ethics of the companies that you work for.

What kind of company?

Take some time to consider the organisational culture that will best suit your working style:

- formal or informal
- fast moving or stable
- secure or risky and exciting
- family friendly or long working hours
- European, American or Asian.

This will help you to get a clear picture of the kind of organisation to focus your search on. The organisations where you can work most effectively will also be the ones that will most want to take you on.

Looking beyond the obvious

Don't narrow down your options unnecessarily. Maybe in the past you have always looked for roles in large corporations with good promotion prospects and job security. Today, there are fewer of those posts and they may not necessarily provide you with the best opportunities. Smaller companies can offer more excitement and challenge, and give you a role that makes you more marketable when you look for your next post. Smaller companies may also be a good option for the older job seeker, as they often cannot afford expensive training programmes and experience is therefore at a premium.

Permanent or temporary?

Don't forget that permanent jobs are not the only option. Consider whether temporary/locum roles or contract work would suit you. Many excellent senior roles are now offered as fixed-term contracts, and working as a contractor may enable you to:

◆ greatly widen your professional **experience**
◆ increase your **marketability** and independence
◆ increase your **earnings** – often dramatically.

In today's world of downsizing and redundancies, a career as a contractor can actually be more secure than one as a permanent employee, if it enables you to increase your marketability and save money against the times when work is slack.

How flexible will you need to be?

The extent to which you are able to pick and choose where you look for work will depend on your personal circumstances and the job market in your professional field.

◆ Do you need to find work quickly, or can you afford to take your time to find a post that is exactly what you want?

◆ Are you tied to a particular location by, for example, family commitments?

◆ Alternatively, do you work in an area so specialised that there are only going to be a few opportunities anywhere in the world and you therefore have to be prepared to go to where the work is?

◆ Or do you work in a field where the jobs market is an embarrassment of riches for skilled people and you can be very choosy about which opportunities you take up?

Think through these issues and make a positive decision about how flexible you will be in your search for work. Identify the boundaries between what you will and what you won't consider. If you are highly marketable, commit to accept only the work that you really want with the kind of organisation that will suit you best. If you are going to have to be more flexible, identify and pursue your ideal but also look at what your 'next best' alternatives are.

If you're just not sure

If you are uncertain about what your goals are in this area of your life, paying for a session with a career consultant is an excellent investment. Their services are not cheap, but your career choices are among the most important decisions that you will ever make. A consultant's fees could well be recouped instantly if they help you win the right job or contract.

DECIDING ON A STRATEGY

Once you know what your goals are in your search for work, you can decide how best to achieve them. As mentioned earlier, you may be able to reach your goals by sending out as many CVs as possible, but this is only likely if:

◆ you are flexible about the roles that you are prepared to accept and the companies that you will work for

◆ you can afford the time to go to a lot of interviews until you find the post you want

◆ there is a large number of organisations which can offer you real career opportunities.

Focusing your search

Most managers and professionals will achieve greater success by making fewer approaches to potential employers, but taking time and trouble to get these approaches right. If you are very senior, or there are only a few organisations offering the kind of work that you are interested in, you will need to spend considerable time and effort researching each possibility and tailoring a CV to fit each organisation that you apply to.

Between these two extremes, an effective strategy is to identify the kind of work and employer which is of most interest to you – for example, you might want a position selling electrical equipment for an international company, or to work as a solicitor in a practice in the Bristol area. Then draw up a CV tailored to those opportunities, and send this off to the organisations which are most likely to be able to provide you with those roles. Take more time over a few CVs to be sent to those employers that you would most like to work for.

In addition, you might decide to use agencies, who will take your CV and make approaches to suitable companies on your behalf. A good agency will be aware of the needs of each of the employers on their books and tailor their approach accordingly, although you will still have to research the company yourself before you attend any interviews.

FINDING THE BEST OPPORTUNITIES

Looking through the job advertisements in the newspaper, professional journals or the internet one way of finding new job opportunities, but a surprising number of vacancies are never advertised in this way. There is a hidden jobs market and many senior posts are filled through:

- job hunters directly approaching the company
- agencies
- head-hunters
- contacts.

You can maximise your chances of success by considering all the options and deciding where you are most likely to find the best opportunities in your field.

Advertisements
The easiest way to find suitable opportunities is often to look through the job ads.

Advantages
- No effort required in finding out where vacancies are.
- You have some information on the vacancy.
- It is easy to compare different opportunities and pick the best.

Disadvantages
- Dozens or even hundreds of others may reply to the same advertisement.
- Many vacancies are never advertised.

Finding the best advertisements
Find out where the best opportunities in your field and at your level are likely to be advertised. This may be:

- national press
- professional journals
- the internet
- trade press.

Make sure that you have access to the best of the advertisements! Ensure that you are on the subscription lists for the best journals in your field, and put a regular order in to your newsagent for the newspapers and magazines that you need. Then block out time in your diary on the day that you get your journal or paper to go through the vacancy pages – if you wait until you have the time you may never get round to it.

Finding vacancies on the internet
The internet gives you instant acess to vacancies around the world. Vacancies can be found on:

◆ internet agency sites such as Monster.co.uk and Totaljobs.com

◆ organisations' home pages

◆ professional associations' web sites

◆ online newspapers and journals, e.g. the online versions of *The Daily Telegraph* and the *Financial Times.*

Some of the best sites at the time of writing are listed in the Useful Addresses section at the back of the book.

There is now such a huge choice of web sites advertising jobs that you may need to do some research into which ones best cover your profession or specialism, before you select a manageable number to use in your jobsearch. It is also worth going straight to the web sites of those organisations which you are most interested in working for, as you may find opportunities advertised here.

The internet has some real advantages for job hunters with limited time. Most sites have a search engine that lets you quickly and easily search through all the listed vacancies for the ones of interest. Even better, some sites let you register your details and then send you an email when suitable vacancies arise.

Deciding whether to apply
One big advantage of advertisements is that the information about the job makes it easy to decide whether it interests you – and whether you would interest the employer. Don't apply if you lack the qualifications or experience that the advertisement stresses are essential... but don't be put off by a daunting list of what the advertisement says are 'desirable' qualities. The critical test, and the one that the employer will apply, is *could you actually do the job*? For example, many advertisements say that 'the candidate will probably be educated to degree level'. In these cases, the recruiter is looking for someone who displays a high level of intelligence and analytical thinking. If you can demonstrate that you have these qualities, it is worth applying for the post even if you did not go to college.

While you obviously need to offer the recruiter a certain level of expertise, do not worry unduly if you lack extensive experience of *all* the aspects of the advertised post. Most employers are looking for someone who will see the job as an exciting challenge.

Getting further information
Most advertisements give the name of someone whom you can ring for further details or an 'informal talk' about the job. Make use of this opportunity; it will give you a chance to find out more about what the employer really wants. Prepare a short list of questions before you call; ask if it is a convenient time to talk; and aim not to take up more than a few minutes of the recruiter's

time. If he or she is happy to talk to you for longer, you should be able to gauge this during your conversation.

The speculative CV

One way of accessing the hidden jobs market is to take the initiative and send out speculative CVs to companies that you know could benefit from your skills and experience.

Advantages

◆ You may put yourself in the running for a job that will never be openly advertised.

◆ You may get access to the company's internal jobs market.

◆ If a post is unadvertised, there will be very few applicants.

◆ Your CV will probably be kept on file for future jobs which come up – and you may therefore be the first that they contact.

◆ If you use email to send your CV out, multiple applications can be made cheaply and easily.

Disadvantage

◆ You may have to send out many CVs to get each interview, which some job hunters find discouraging.

Finding the best opportunities

The internet allows you to send large numbers of CVs out with very little effort. Some job hunters find the scattergun approach of emailing hundreds of CVs is adequate for their needs. The disadvantage of this casual strategy – particularly for more senior job hunters – is that you may waste time following through applications to organisations which cannot offer you real career progression, while overlooking the best opportunities. Take some time to identify the organisations which are most likely to offer the very best opportunities. Look for companies that are:

◆ expanding their market share or number of clients

◆ being awarded large new orders or contracts

◆ opening new outlets/offices

◆ branching out into your field of expertise

◆ changing the way in which they do business

◆ going through a phase in their development where your specialist skills could add value (for example, exporting abroad for the first time, or introducing an IT system in which you are an expert).

Make the most of your sources of information. Your professional/ trade organisation and journal, the business press, specialist web sites and your network of contacts will give valuable news about what organisations in your field are doing.

Finding out more
Once you have identified a company that looks like it could provide you with opportunities, spend some time doing research. As a manager or professional, you will need to show that:

◆ you understand the challenges and concerns of the organisation that you are applying to

◆ you can help the organisation succeed in dealing with these challenges.

The more senior you are, the more you will be expected to know about the firms you apply to.

Good sources of information are:

- the company's web site
- annual reports
- the business press and internet sites
- your network of contacts – who may be able to tell you the truth behind the glossy annual report.

The organisation's website may even be advertising a post of interest to you! Don't assume that any vacancy listing they are publishing is complete. Many organisations do not publish their most senior vacancies on the web; searches for staff are often undertaken very discreetly; and things can move so fast in a company that even their own website cannot keep up.

The recruitment section of a web site can also give useful information as to where speculative CVs can be sent.

Calling the company
Most larger companies strongly encourage speculative CVs to be sent to one central email account, which enables them to be efficiently processed. Take advantage of this facility; it will often enable you to get your CV onto the organisation's central database so that they can contact you if a suitable vacancy arises. However, you may also want to make a more personal approach to selected individual(s) within the company. The advantages of making a direct approach are:

- you can contact the line manager direct; in larger organisations most speculative CVs are filtered out by the HR department

- if the manager has spoken to you personally, they are more likely to read your CV than if it arrives from a completely unknown individual

- you have the opportunity to make a positive impression during your call.

If you have not been able to identify the individual that you need to talk to from your contacts, the company's switchboard should be able to put you through to a suitable manager in the right department.

Leaving the right impression
Remember that the aim of your first contact with an employer – whether by phone or in person – is simply to introduce yourself and perhaps to gain a little information . Try to leave the manager with a positive impression rather than attempt to talk them into giving you a job. Aim to limit the conversation to a couple of minutes, unless it becomes obvious that they are willing to talk for longer.

If the employer urgently needs someone with your experience they can always ask you more questions during the conversation. Otherwise, you can send them a CV that they can look at when they have the time. If your CV is not successful initially, you may want to call again in a few months' time when the situation might have changed. However, unless you have specifically been asked to, do not continue to cold call the same organisation as they are unlikely to welcome this!

Applying to agencies

A good agency will take your CV, find vacancies that would suit you and then market you to relevant organisations.

Advantages

◆ Agencies often have access to the unadvertised jobs market.

◆ Agencies may act as head-hunters.

◆ Agencies will market you to the companies that use them.

◆ Using an agency is free to the applicant – they make their money through charging the companies that use their services.

Disadvantages

◆ Agencies may try to make commission by persuading you to accept a post that you don't really want.

◆ Not all agencies are reputable.

◆ You may need to apply to a number of agencies, especially if you want to do temporary or contract work on a long-term basis.

Approaching agencies

Approach an agency as you would a potential employer. Take some time to select the ones that will do the best job for you – those that specialise in your field and/or senior posts and that have a good reputation. Agencies that are members of the Recruitment and Employment Confederation (REC) have to reach the Confederation's approved standards.

You may come into contact with an agency because they are advertising a specific job that you are interested in, or you may decide to make a direct contact. In either case, call the agent before sending your CV in. This introduces you to them in person, and the agent may be able to give you more information about the jobs that they have on offer. Don't be surprised, however, if they are not very forthcoming over the phone. They may be discreet either on the instructions of clients or because they are concerned that you might be a rival agency.

Make an effort to leave the agent with a positive impression, just as you would if you were dealing directly with an employer. Reputable agents make their money by supplying companies with high-calibre staff and will take more time over marketing the services of those they are convinced would make quality employees or contractors. Supply a carefully prepared CV and treat your agent with courtesy. If they persistently call you with attempts to make you attend interviews or accept posts, remember that they are working just as hard to persuade employers to take you on. Of course, you may send off your CV to the agency and hear nothing. In this case call again to find out what has happened – agencies often receive hundreds or even thousands of CVs every week and yours may have gone astray.

Preparing a CV for an agency
When you send an application to an agency, you seldom know at the outset who will see your CV. Even if you are replying to a specific job advertisement that the agency has placed, they may not immediately give the name of the company that they are acting for. The agency may also want to consider your application for other vacancies on their books. For these reasons, be careful not to tailor your CV too closely to one particular job or employer when sending an application to an agency.

Rogue agencies

Finally, a few words of warning. A few agencies are less than reputable or competent, so beware of the following:

♦ Don't pay an agency to find you work. The recruiting company should pay the agency, with the service being free to the applicant.

♦ Don't allow yourself to be tied to one agency. Any reputable agency will understand that you want to use several agencies to give yourself the best possible chance of finding work.

♦ Don't hand in your notice to your current employer until you have a new contract signed, even if the agency tries to persuade you that they can guarantee you work.

Making the most of your contacts

If you are a mature and experienced manager or professional, your contacts may be your best way of finding work. Cultivate good relationships with those in your trade or professional organisation, clients, suppliers and even your ex-employers. Discreetly let them know that you are interested in opportunities outside your current role, and they may be able to tell you about vacancies, pass on news about which firms are due to expand or have just won new contracts – or even offer you a post.

Don't forget that the internet offers chances to network online. Look for online communities relevant to your job search. For example, Monster.co.uk has online communities of job hunters who exchange information on employers and vacancies.

Find ways of enhancing your reputation outside your current firm, perhaps by speaking at conferences, publishing papers or taking part in the programmes run by your professional organisation. You are more likely to get work from someone who knows and respects you, and you may attract the notice of a head-hunter.

Always make sure that you have a supply of up-to-date CVs so that you can respond immediately to any opportunities that present themselves.

Working with a head-hunter

Head-hunters search for individuals to fill senior posts where the company has to be discreet about the recruitment process, or where they want to make contact with people who are not actively looking for another role. By their very nature they will usually contact you rather than the other way round. However, if you are aware of a good head-hunter in your field you may wish to make contact with them to let them know that you are looking for another role.

When you send your CV to a head-hunter you may not initially be aware of the role which they are considering you for. However, you should be able to glean a good deal of general information from the head-hunter about the nature of the job and this will help you in tailoring your CV to suit the opportunity on offer. The head-hunter will often give you an initial interview before deciding whether to forward your CV to the company which they are working for. If they decide to forward your CV, they should always gain your permission for this in advance and at this stage let you know the organisation they are recruiting for. Work closely with the head-hunter; it is usually in their best interests financially to help you negotiate a good salary package and even if your application for one particular role is not successful they may well become aware of other opportunities in the future.

CASE STUDIES
Steve

Steve is a 42-year-old systems analyst. He is divorced and has no particular ties to any area of the country. For the last seven years Steve has been travelling around the UK working on a variety of short-term contracts, and he has lately come to feel that he would like a more settled lifestyle. Because of his highly marketable skills, he has literally hundreds of opportunities to choose from. He pays for a day with a career consultant to clarify his professional goals. As a result, he decides to focus on looking for project management contracts, as this is the part of his work that he enjoys most. He also decides to buy a house in Yorkshire and look for contracts within commuting distance of his new home.

Steve already has good working relationships with a number of specialist IT agencies that have found work for him in the past. He lets them know the direction in which he now wants to develop his career, and revamps his CV accordingly. He also starts to visit regularly sites on the internet that advertise suitable work.

Sue

Sue is a 32-year-old maintenance manager. Since completing a degree in building surveying, she has managed the maintenance of major office developments. She now wants to expand her skills by taking on a facility manager's role, managing not just maintenance but all the other services that an office needs to run smoothly, such as security and catering. Because she has a small child, she doesn't want to commute long distances but she knows that there will be very few suitable vacancies in the area where she lives.

Sue knows that her chances of success will be limited if she sends out speculative CVs at random. Because even the largest companies only employ a handful of facilities managers, the chances of a vacancy coinciding with receipt of a speculative CV are small. She therefore identifies:

◆ the facilities management contractors who manage developments in her local area

◆ companies building or moving into new developments locally.

She makes a list of the five most promising prospects, and researches each one thoroughly in order to make an impressive approach to each with a speculative CV. She has worked with managers in a couple of the companies and they are able to give her some useful information on possible vacancies and the best way to approach each company.

Brian

Brian is 51. He left school without qualifications and spent several years doing a variety of clerical jobs until he found his niche in the personnel department of British Engineering. He has spent the rest of his career with the company, building his experience and enjoying steady progression until he reached the level of human resources manager. British Engineering is now downsizing, and Brian knows that he will shortly be made redundant. Brian is concerned that his age and one-company career will count against him in his search for a job.

At first, Brian applied for jobs as close as possible to his current one – permanent posts in the human resources departments of large corporations. However, he found that he was getting very few interviews. Brian's outplacement consultant suggests that he should consider taking on temporary and contract work, and that he should make the most of his large network of contacts.

Brian is active in the local branch of his professional association and is well respected there. He is able to informally approach a number of people in his field to find out whether permanent or temporary vacancies are likely to come up in their companies. Brian has been responsible for running the human resources IT systems at work, and he lets his regular contact at the company that supplied the software know that he is looking for a job. He also talks to the suppliers of the training materials that his company uses, and the consultants who have been running special projects for them.

CHECKLIST

◆ Can you define the kind of work that you want?

◆ Can you define the kind of company you want to work for?

◆ Do you know where to find the best advertisements?

◆ Are there any companies that it would be worth making a speculative approach to?

◆ Have you researched the best opportunities?

◆ Do you know which are the best agencies in your field?

◆ Can you list all the contacts who might be able to help you?

POINTS TO CONSIDER

1. Would you be better applying for a permanent job in a large corporation – or developing your career using a less traditional route such as employment in locum positions and small firms?

2. Are you more likely to be successful if you make a large number of applications, or if you make a smaller number but spend more time over each application?

3. How are you most likely to find out about the best opportunities in your field?

(2)

Finding Your Key Selling Points

Your CV is not your autobiography. It is not even a detailed career history. It is your personal sales brochure, created to persuade the employer that you have what their organisation needs and that they should take the time to meet you and find out more. For this reason, your CV should concentrate on your **key selling points** – the reasons why the employer would want to take you on.

Invest time in working out:

◆ what the employer is looking for
◆ what you have to offer
◆ how to present this information for maximum impact.

FINDING OUT WHAT THE EMPLOYER NEEDS

The recruiter will be looking for an individual who has:

◆ the right technical **skills/experience**
◆ a high level of **interpersonal skills**
◆ the ability to flourish within the company **culture**
◆ at the most senior levels – the ability to **shape** the company culture.

Every employer will be looking for people with excellent technical skills and experience. For managerial and professional employees in particular, they also look for someone with the right personality and working style for the company.

Looking at what the organisation values

Each individual industry and company values different traits in their employees. A civil service organisation will need people who can work within fixed structures and procedures. A new high-tech company will be looking for people who can cope with fast, unpredictable change. A small and stable company with few promotion opportunities may well look for someone who is content to stay within the same role for a number of years. A rapidly expanding firm will need someone who can grow and change with them ... and so on.

At a senior level, a company may look for someone who does not fit comfortably into the existing culture of the organisation. They may deliberately seek out someone with a different way of working, who will bring in fresh ideas and shake the place up. Bear this in mind when you are applying to a company that you know is aiming to:

- expand
- improve their products and services
- improve their customer service, financial management, etc.
- reduce bureaucracy
- increase flexibility and speed of response
- change the organisational culture.

Researching employers

To get a clear picture of what the recruiter will be looking for, start by researching the organisation or industry's:

- goals
- challenges

- opportunities
- culture
- competitors.

Consider the environment that the organisation is working within. Are they facing challenges and opportunities with, for example, new technology, changing tax regulations or forthcoming legislation?

Advertisements provide direct information on what an individual employer wants and often more subtle clues as well. A company describing itself as 'well established, with prestigious clients' is likely to be very different from one that has placed an advertisement asking for people to work in 'exciting new opportunities'.

What does the organisation need?
Your research will enable you to identify what the organisation is trying to achieve and what kind of people they need to get them there. They may need, for example, people who can:

- maintain and build on existing relationships with clients

- pursue a policy of aggressive competition with competitors

- change the culture of the organisation

- introduce procedures and processes to ensure that the organisation runs smoothly.

What does the team need?
If you are very interested in working for a particular organisation, see if your contacts can tell you about the team that you would be

working with. Successful teams need a mixture of individuals and they may have a particular need for someone who can, for example:

◆ generate new ideas
◆ ensure that plans are followed through to completion
◆ check that details are correct
◆ take a leadership role.

ASSETS EVERY EMPLOYER NEEDS

Some qualities will be an asset to someone looking for almost any senior post.

Strategic thinking

At a senior level, you will be expected to demonstrate an understanding of the broader issues, opportunities and challenges facing the organisation and its wider environment. Employers are looking for people who can visualise ways in which the company can move forward taking all these factors into account. Business acumen and/or professional judgement are vital.

Change orientation

Even the most traditional organisations are having to adapt at an ever-increasing speed. You will need to demonstrate that you thrive on change and constantly look for ways in which to improve the way your organisation works. This will usually involve an ability to:

◆ challenge assumptions
◆ take calculated risks
◆ demonstrate resilience and tenacity.

Creativity

Linked to the need to change is the need to come up with new and better solutions, products and ways of working.

Quality orientation

At a senior level, you need to be able to demonstrate not just your personal ability to deliver high-quality work, but your ability to shape the organisation to deliver excellent results.

Leadership ability

Employers need people who not only manage staff, but motivate and inspire them to achieve the organisation's goals.

Interpersonal skills

An ability to get on with people is going to be an advantage at any level. Senior people need to demonstrate personal impact and an ability to develop and manage relationships effectively. You will need to show that you can influence and motivate others and work successfully in high-profile or difficult situations. For example, you may need to show that you can resolve conflict, negotiate, manage teams split over a number of different locations, or make presentations to customers at board level.

Communication skills

Employers need people who are confident and effective communicators in both speech and writing. Senior people need to be able to use communication to persuade and influence others.

Personal management skills

In today's de-layered organisations, employers are looking for people who can manage themselves. You will need to show self-motivation, self-reliance and an ability to develop your own career.

Integrity

This goes without saying. Make sure your CV is honest!

Case study – Brian investigates Zipco

Brian is interested in a vacancy for a training manager that he has seen in a human resources magazine (see Figure 1).

Brian analyses the advertisement

From the advertisement, Brian can see that Zipco are looking for someone with technical skills and experience in the following areas:

- delivery of management and technical development initiatives
- design and delivery of internal training initiatives
- management of external training providers
- development of people at all levels of the organisation
- operating within the high-tech manufacturing sector
- working on their own initiative and motivating themselves.

They would *like* this person to be a graduate and a member of the Chartered Institute of Personnel and Development, but it appears that the recruiter doesn't see these points as *essential*.

Brian also concludes that as the training manager will be working as part of a small human resources team, it will be important that the person Zipco takes on does not have a narrow focus on development, but understands the role of HR as a whole.

Brian sums up Zipco's values

The language used in the advertisement gives a clear picture of Zipco's values:

ZIPCO

Training Manager – Gleneagle, Scotland
(Ref. XXXXX)
9-month contract (maternity leave cover)

Zipco is an exciting new information technology company established in 1998. Commitment to innovation and product excellence is leading to year-on-year growth in this fast-moving and competitive sector. Our Gleneagle assembly plant plays a vital role in the company's strategy. This high-tech site employs 500 people, ranging from skilled assembly staff to R&D specialists.

We are looking for an experienced professional to cover the role of Training Manager. Working as part of a small Human Resources team, you will manage the delivery of management and technical development initiatives, using both in-house and external providers.

You will be able to demonstrate a track record of successful training management in a high-tech manufacturing environment. Self-motivated and innovative, you will have the highest professional standards and will probably be a graduate and a member of the Chartered Institute of Personnel and Development.

If you can meet this challenge, please send your CV to Michael Black, Resourcing Consultant, Palmer and Cornwell International, 103 Park Street, Edinburgh (Phone 5555 – 666 – 77777) **michael@rescan.co.uk**.

Fig. 1. An example of an advertisement.

- ◆ exciting
- ◆ new
- ◆ innovation
- ◆ product excellence
- ◆ growth
- ◆ fast-moving
- ◆ competitive.

Brian researches further

Brian speaks to the consultant who is handling recruitment to this role, reads through company website and talks to contacts in the Association of Engineering Employers who deal with Zipco. He finds out that the company is owned by a multinational with American origins. They are pursuing an aggressive policy of expanding their business by designing products that are one step ahead of what their competitors produce. The company is new, change is constant, and staff who cannot deliver results are quickly discarded.

Brian soon learns that the rapid pace of change within Zipco has caused some problems. The provision of training and development has been haphazard, which has sometimes led to an unacceptable level of defects in their finished products. The company recognises this and realises that improvements need to be made, which is why the post of training manager was recently created.

Brian measures himself against the advertisement

Brian has not been working in the same competitive and fast-moving environment as Zipco – his current employer, British Engineering, is a more traditional manufacturing company. However, he has the right skills and experience to enable him to make an immediate contribution, and he can also offer something that Zipco tends to lack – the ability to put systems and procedures in place.

IDENTIFYING YOUR KEY SELLING POINTS

Once you have identified what the organisation or industry that you are applying to wants from their employees, you can work out your key selling points – the main reasons why they will want to employ you. These may include your:

◆ relevant experience
◆ relevant qualifications
◆ track record of previous successes
◆ personal attributes
◆ motivation.

These are the main areas that you will want to advertise to the recruiter, and the basis of your CV.

Proving you have what it takes

Look at how you can prove to the recruiter that you have these qualities. You can't just say that you are experienced, tenacious, or have business acumen – you must prove it through your achievements. For example, if you have excellent negotiating skills, you must give details of the negotiations that you have successfully concluded and the resulting benefits for your company. Wherever possible, the proof must be work related. Only new graduates and junior staff can use their hobbies and interests as the main evidence for their abilities.

Case study – Steve identifies his key selling points

Steve has done a wide variety of IT contract work. Most of this has been systems analysis, but during the last few years he has managed a number of IT projects and he now wants to specialise in this area. He knows that recruiting companies want people with:

◆ good technical skills and experience of successfully completing projects

◆ the commitment to finish jobs to a high standard, within budget and to the set deadline

◆ an ability to reach a full understanding of the needs of a company and to put in place systems that fill these needs

◆ good interpersonal skills, so that the consultant can work effectively with the staff in the client company.

Steve therefore identifies his key selling points as follows:

◆ **Relevant qualifications and experience** – with a variety of blue-chip companies and a range of IT systems and packages.

◆ **Track record of previous successes** – in managing several large projects from start to finish and to his clients' standards and deadlines.

◆ **Motivation and ability** – to solve complex business problems and put into place systems that meet his clients' needs.

◆ **Personal attributes** – good interpersonal skills. Steve is good at dealing with others in client companies. He is an excellent trainer and before he finishes a project, he makes sure that everyone is happy with using the new system.

Steve can provide *evidence* of his key selling points as follows:

◆ **Relevant experience** – he can list the blue-chip companies he has worked for and all the systems and packages that he is an expert on. For *example: Implementing an Ameritech-based payroll system for 5,000 staff at Supercorp UK.*

◆ **Qualifications** – Steve has an engineering degree and is a chartered engineer.

◆ **Track record of previous successes** – he can give details of the major projects that he has managed, and the fact that he completed the projects within the clients' deadlines, to their quality standards and within budget. For example: *Redeveloping a customer information database to a tight deadline for the Clothesco mail order company. Migrating the records of 20,000 customers from an ITCO to a Megatech platform; improving data quality control methods (e.g. error reporting and change control) to improve accuracy of records and reduce customer complaints.*

◆ **Motivation to solve complex business problems** – when describing the projects that he has managed, Steve can tell the recruiter about the issues that the company was facing and how the solution that he devised helped. For example: *Designing and implementing a secure company intranet system to improve the speed of data access, reduce paperwork and ensure that data is up to date.*

◆ **Good interpersonal skills** – Steve has trained the users of his systems and ensured a smooth handover to the client company.

Exercise
List the five main reasons why an employer would want to recruit you. For each of these selling points, write down how you can prove these qualities.

What other strengths should you make the recruiter aware of?
What evidence of these strengths can you offer the recruiter?

DEALING WITH WEAKNESSES

Once you have identified your strengths, have a think about which
points a recruiter reading your CV might see as weaknesses. These
could be:

◆ gaps in skills, knowledge or experience
◆ lack of qualifications
◆ a career path with breaks or long periods of irrelevant
  experience
◆ many employers
◆ only having worked for one employer.

Is the gap too wide?

If looking at your weaknesses reveals a serious mismatch between
the needs of the employer and what you can offer, your
application will probably be wasted. Reconsider your options. Are
you more likely to be successful with applications to other
companies or for a different type of work? Or is there action that
you could take to bridge the gap, perhaps by taking further
qualifications or gaining more experience?

It is more likely that your weaknesses are no greater than those
that most job hunters have. Recruiters never see candidates who
are perfect in every detail! Often perceived weaknesses simply
reflect the fact that your background or career path is not typical
for your industry or profession. It is important, however, that you
recognise where a recruiter might see a problem, and that you
decide how to deal with this in your CV.

Your options are:

- Turn what might be perceived as a weakness to your advantage by showing the recruiter the benefits of your particular set of experiences.

- Find strengths that offset your weaknesses.

- Write your CV in such a way that the weaker points are not emphasised.

The examples in the following questions and answers show how this can be done.

Question and answer session

'It's clear from the advertisement that they are looking for a graduate. I know that I could do the job, but I don't have a degree. How do I handle this?'

There are relatively few jobs for which a degree is really essential. Usually a recruiter is simply looking for someone with a certain level of intelligence and analytical thinking. Offset the lack of a degree by emphasising your abilities, experience and business acumen. Move the Education and Training section of your CV to the end of the document, so the recruiter only reads this after they have seen what you have to offer.

'I want to work in an area of the finance industry that is very traditional – even staid. I'm worried that employers are going to think that the banks I have worked for previously are downmarket. Aren't they going to conclude that I couldn't possibly fit in?'

If you are of a different background from most of an organisation's employees, you can bring in new ideas and a fresh perspective. Your CV should show the *benefits* that your experience could bring to your chosen employer. For example, with your background you might be in an ideal position to spot where bureaucracy should be reduced or how the customer base could be widened. Show that you can easily adapt to different situations – perhaps you have worked abroad, or in a number of very different roles.

'This job is a big step up from where I am at the moment. How am I going to get them to take my application seriously?'

Emphasise that this post would be an exciting challenge for you. Most employers are looking for someone who wants to learn and develop rather than someone who could do the job blindfold (and who might therefore get bored). Show through your past achievements that you have the *ability* to do this job, and that you have successfully taken on difficult challenges in the past.

'I've worked for a large number of employers. Aren't they going to think that I can't stick with any job for long?'

If you've worked in a large number of roles you have a broad range of experience, and are probably adaptable and full of new ideas. Sell these benefits! Your CV should, however, show a logical career pattern rather than a series of apparently random job moves. For example, you may have taken on the same kind of work for a wide variety of different employers, worked in a number of different roles to build up a range of experience within one particular industry, or changed to a career which better fitted your aptitudes.

Exercise

List three points that a recruiter reading your CV might see as weaknesses, and decide how you will deal with these points in your CV.

CHECKLIST

◆ Have you sufficiently researched the employer or industry that you are applying to?

◆ Can you define the challenges and opportunities that they are facing?

◆ Do you have a feel for the company or industry culture?

◆ Can you list the benefits that you can bring to the organisation?

◆ Are you aware of anything that a recruiter might see as a problem?

◆ Have you decided how you will deal with this?

POINTS TO CONSIDER

1. If you were a recruiter, what would you want candidates to offer?

2. If you were a recruiter, what would make you think that a candidate was unsuitable?

3. Has the exercise of defining your strengths and weaknesses given you ideas on how you could enhance your employability?

3

Selling Yourself

Once you have worked out your key selling points you know **what** you want to say to the recruiter. However, in order to sell yourself effectively you need to plan **how** you are going to present this information.

Your CV is your personal marketing document – an advertisement for yourself. Advertisers make sure that they catch the eye of the reader, they use evocative language, and they make sure that the reader understands the benefits of buying the product. Taking the same approach with your CV will maximise the impact that it has on the reader. This is particularly important for senior CVs. You are not just showing the recruiter that you have a certain set of skills and experiences, but persuading them that you can make a real and positive impact on the organisation that you join.

This does not mean, of course, that your CV should exaggerate your ability or mislead the recruiter in any way. Your aim should be to help the recruiter by making sure that they fully understand what you genuinely have to offer their organisation. You can do this by:

◆ concentrating on the points that will be important to the recruiter

◆ presenting your skills, experience and achievements in a way that does them full justice.

GETTING YOUR MESSAGE OVER

Your first aim is to make sure that your CV gets read. Recruiters are busy people. They will usually give each CV a quick scan, pick the best for a more thorough reading, and pick only the very best of those to invite for an interview. Speculative CVs may receive only a cursory glance, especially if they have arrived out of the blue without a preliminary contact being made first (see Chapter 1). It is therefore vital for your CV to make it absolutely clear to the most perfunctory reader what you can offer them.

This means that your CV should be short. Keeping your CV short means that your key selling points really stand out, instead of being buried in a mass of less interesting facts. A good rule of thumb is:

- one A4 page for speculative CVs
- two pages for most applications
- three pages for applications for very senior jobs.

Question and answer session

'I have thirty years' experience! How on earth am I going to put this on to one or two pages?'

By concentrating on your current key selling points rather than documenting the entire 30 years. The aim of a CV is to get an interview, and you only need include information that is going to help you get that interview. Once you are talking to the employer, you will have the opportunity to fill in any missing details.

'So what can I leave out of a CV?'

The following information can usually be left out of a CV:

- marital status
- numbers and ages of children
- details of jobs held more than fifteen years ago
- minute details of more recent jobs
- details of your junior schools
- irrelevant, obsolete or lower-level qualifications, e.g. GCSEs if you have a PhD
- failed examinations
- reasons for leaving jobs
- salary details
- hobbies and interests (unless directly relevant)
- place of birth
- nationality
- age
- details of your referees
- names of relatives already working for the organisation. This looks unprofessional on a senior CV.

'But I thought that recruiters didn't like to see unexplained gaps in CVs. What do I do about giving information on jobs I held twenty or thirty years ago?'

Employers don't like it if you leave months or years in your career unaccounted for. It might mean that you were in prison! Give brief details of your early jobs; for example, *1970–1975 Developing experience as a journalist on a number of local papers.*

MAKING A POWERFUL FIRST IMPRESSION

First impressions count. If your CV starts with a powerful selling point that catches the recruiter's eye, they are likely to read further to find out all about you. If you start off with irrelevant information or something that could be construed as a weakness, the recruiter may not take the time to read your CV and find out what you have to offer. Even if they do read it, a negative first impression colours the way that a recruiter sees the rest of your CV.

For most people the first and main section of their CV should therefore deal with their employment history, as this is the crucial area that shows whether they can do the job on offer. At a senior level, the exception to this would be CVs for jobs where qualifications are of paramount importance; for example, academics and research scientists.

Putting first things first

As you prepare each section of your CV, keep in mind the principle that first impressions count. Put details of your most impressive or relevant achievements at the top of each section. For example, you should usually put details of your current or last job at the top of your Career and Achievements section and then work through previous posts in reverse chronological order. In the information on your current job your most eye-catching achievement should come first – and so on.

Ending on a high note

End your CV on a high note so that you leave the reader with a final positive image of you as they put the CV down. A section on your interesting hobbies or the languages that you speak can be a good way of ending a CV.

Case study – Brian reorders his CV

Brian is amused to find a CV that he prepared for himself a number of years ago. The first page is shown in Figure 2.

CURRICULUM VITAE

PERSONAL DETAILS

NAME: Brian Arthur White

ADDRESS: 62 Fenn Road,
              Hawley,
              Kent,
              LB7 8PG

TEL: 0234-567890 (Home)
              0234-876543 (Office)

D.O.B: 12th January 1956

PLACE OF BIRTH: Coshall, Cheshire
NATIONALITY: British

MARITAL STATUS: Married with two daughters

EDUCATION

Sep '65 – June '71 Coshall School, Coshall, Cheshire (I was given the opportunity of a good job with my father's firm, and so left before taking my exams).

EMPLOYMENT HISTORY

Feb '71 – Jan '72 – Trainee Clerical Assistant, Westforth and Sons Engineering, Coshall, Cheshire.
Unfortunately, the job did not turn out as planned and so I left to go to a better firm.

Jan '72 – Sept '73 – Trainee Clerk, Personnel and Welfare Department, Coshall Bus Company, Coshall, Cheshire.
I gained a thorough training in all aspects of clerical work within Personnel.

Fig. 2. Page one of Brian's old CV.

While most of the information on it is still accurate, he winces to think of the first impression that it would give if he used it today:

- I haven't got any paper qualifications.
- I can offer clerical experience.
- I've got two daughters who could well be in the middle of important exams making relocation a problem.

Brian has excellent skills and experience as a human resources manager, but a recruiter might not turn to the second page of his CV to find out what he has to offer their organisation. Compare this to the CV that Brian has put together today (see Figure 3).

Right from the start, this CV gives the recruiter all the reasons why he should see Brian for an interview. The first page concentrates on:

- How the recruiter can contact Brian.

- Brian's most recent and relevant career achievements. In this CV, he has not wasted space on his early years in clerical jobs. Brian has given detailed information about the last fifteen years of his career, and has briefly summarised his earlier experience.

- The skills and experience Brian has to offer.

PRESENTING YOUR EXPERIENCE FOR MAXIMUM IMPACT

Advertisers take a lot of care in preparing the description of their product. You should do the same when describing yourself in your CV. Make sure that you do yourself justice in the way that you describe yourself in your CV:

BRIAN WHITE
87 Chambers Walk, Crawton, Surrey, GT7 9XQ
Telephone: 01234-567890 (Home) 01234-876543 (mobile)
email: bw@interet.co.uk

Profile

A Human Resources Manager with a wide range of experience in the engineering industry. An expert in providing the full range of personnel and training services, including compensation and benefits, industrial relations and payroll management.

Career and Achievements to Date

British Engineering (Aeronautical Division) Crawton, Surrey

The Aeronautical Division of BE has 400 employees in the design and manufacture of sophisticated electrical systems used in civilian aircraft. The division is based on a greenfield site and annual turnover is £100 million.

Human Resources Manager (March XX – Present)
- Reporting to the Director and General Manager, managing a team of up to five staff to provide a full Human Resources support service to the Aeronautical Division.

- Devising and implementing HR strategies to support the Division in meeting its business aims of quality improvement and the introduction of new manufacturing processes. Providing compensation and benefits, industrial relations, training, recruitment, HR systems and payroll management.

- Managing the downsizing of the workforce from 600 to 400 staff in a unionised environment without industrial action or disruption to production. Handling redundancies, redeployment and transfers of staff.

- Negotiating the introduction of new working patterns and compensation systems, to support the introduction of new manufacturing processes.

Fig. 3. Brian's new time-based CV.

Training Manager (Feb XX – Feb XX)
- Liaising with the management team to analyse development needs for the Division, and implement effective training solutions.

- Meeting the Division's need to improve the technical skills of manufacturing staff with the introduction of training to NVQ standards. This has contributed to a 12% fall in the number of units rejected during quality inspection.

British Engineering Motor Components Ltd Petersham, Cambs

BEMC employs 3,000 staff based over four sites in the south and midlands.

Personnel Manager (July XX – Feb XX)
- Reporting to the Personnel Director, managing a team of three staff to provide a full Personnel and Administration support service to the Petersham site.
- Managing industrial relations, moving from a culture of conflict towards more effective working relationships.

Previous Experience

I built up experience in a variety of Personnel and Training roles within a number of British Engineering companies between September XXXX and February XXXX. This experience included:
- Designing and delivering management, interpersonal skills, and induction courses to staff at all levels.
- Providing a generalist Personnel service.

Between February XXXX and September XXXX I built up experience in a variety of clerical jobs in Coshall, Cheshire.

Interests
I am a keen runner and cyclist. I enjoy taking part in fun runs and charity cycle rides.

Additional Information

- Willing to relocate within the UK and travel worldwide
- Clean, full driving licence
- Health – excellent
- References available on request.

Fig. 3. (contd).

- back up the claims that you make
- quantify your achievements
- show that you can deliver what is most important in your job
- use positive and powerful language
- avoid meaningless 'puff' and padding
- avoid ambiguous language
- avoid jargon
- be professional.

Backing up your claims

Which of these examples has more credibility?

'I am an excellent leader and build high performance teams'

or

'On taking up the post of European sales manager, I set up a team of ten salespeople based in three EU countries. By focusing on communication, motivation and goal setting, we exceeded demanding sales targets in each of the four years that I held this post.'

It is not enough to say that you have a particular skill or quality – for example, that you are an excellent communicator or an expert on taxation. Help the recruiter to understand fully what you have to offer them by providing evidence. For example:

- give examples of what you have achieved in the past

- show where you have overcome difficult challenges in making these achievements

- quantify your achievements where possible

- tell the reader how your organisation benefited.

Your aim is to prove to the recruiter through your past achievements that you have what it takes to succeed within their organisation.

Quantifying achievements

Quantifying your achievements gives a more meaningful picture of the size of your role and what you achieved within it. For example:

◆ *Staff Nurse Grade D on the Acute Female Surgical Ward (30 beds).*

◆ *Managing the accounts of 50 customers.*

Where possible, you should quantify any improvements that you have made, for example:

◆ *Saved the department £30,000 over 12 months.*

◆ *Increased first-time test passes by 10%.*

Think about the best way to quantify your achievements. Perhaps you only dealt with two clients at a time, but over your ten years with the firm you successfully handled projects for over 100 clients, and had numerous repeat orders from satisfied customers. Putting the information that way gives a much clearer picture of what you achieved.

Showing that you can deliver what is most important in your job

For many jobs, numbers can only ever give part of the picture. How do you show that you are, for example, a caring social worker, a talented designer or an inspiring teacher? You may be able to show an increase in exam passes or your involvement in extra-curricular activities as evidence, but much of your ability will be conveyed in the way in which you talk about your job. This should show that you understand which elements of your work are important and that you take pride in doing these well.

Case study – Steve shows he knows what is important to his clients

In describing his past achievements, Steve can use some impressive statistics. For example, he has:

- implemented projects with a value of up to £1 million
- redeveloped a customer information database holding 20,000 customer records
- implemented a payroll system covering 5,000 staff.

Steve knows that this doesn't tell the whole story. When he writes his CV, he includes the following points:

- the projects were completed to clients' time, budget and quality standards

- the projects met his clients' ultimate goals – for example, reducing customer complaints or increasing the speed of data access

- ongoing support was provided where needed.

By doing this, Steve is showing that he knows how important these points are to clients, and that he makes sure that he delivers in these areas.

Using positive and powerful language

Your CV should use clear and positive language. The following may provide inspiration for describing your achievements:

Ability	Eliminating	Persuading
Accurate	Enabling	Planning
Achieving	Enforcing	Preparing
Adapting	Ensuring	Preventing
Administering	Establishing	Professional
Advising	Evaluating	Profit
Analysing	Exceeding	Promoted
Appraising	Experienced	Promoting
Appropriate	Flexibility	Providing
Approving	Forecasting	Proving
Arranging	Forming	Publishing
Assessing	Founding	Purchasing
Auditing	Gaining	Qualified
Averting	Generating	Quality
Avoiding	Goals	Quantifying
Awareness	Guiding	Raising
Building	Heading	Recruiting
Centralising	Impact	Redesigning
Challenging	Implementing	Reducing
Clients	Improving	Reorganising
Coaching	Increasing	Representing
Communicating	Independently	Researching
Completing	Influencing	Resolving
Conducting	Initiating	Results
Consolidating	Initiative	Reviewing
Constructing	Interpreting	Revising
Constructive	Introducing	Saving
Convincing	Investigating	Scheduling
Co-ordinating	Judgement	Securing
Cost savings	Launching	Selling
Creating	Leading	Significant
Customers	Liaising	Solving
Deadlines	Maintaining	Standardising
Decentralising	Managing	Strategic
Deciding	Marketing	Streamlining
Delegating	Mediating	Successful
Delivering	Modelling	Supporting
Demonstrating	Modernising	Teambuilding
Designing	Monitoring	Team working
Developing	Motivating	Testing
Diagnosing	Negotiating	Training
Directing	Objectives	Upgrading
Displaying	Operating	Validating
Documenting	Organising	Versatile

Avoiding 'puff'

Don't fill your CV with meaningless puff and the latest business buzzwords. Claims such as 'Dynamic high-achiever with track record of success in business process re-engineering' sound false and give little real information to the recruiter.

Use these words with caution when describing yourself:

◆ *Achiever, dynamic* and *inspiring* sound pretentious.

◆ *Excellent* and *successful* can be overused – count up the number of times they appear in your CV.

◆ It goes without saying that senior people should be *reliable, hardworking, honest* and *conscientious*.

◆ The language that you use should support your professional image. Words like *friendly* or *helpful* are too soft and are best avoided by senior people.

Avoiding padding

My duties included managing the Chiswick branch . . .
During this time, I was responsible for family law cases . . .

Phrases like 'duties included' and 'during this time' add nothing to the information that follows. Use bullet points and start each bullet point with a strong verb. This style avoids the constant repetition of the words 'I' and 'my'. For example:

Achievements
◆ *Managing the Chiswick Branch . . .*
◆ *Responsible for family law cases . . .*

Avoiding ambiguity

I worked as one of a small team of managers...
I supported the change process...
I participated in the polymers research project...
I assisted with financial planning for the company...

These phrases leave the recruiter none the wiser as to what you were actually doing. Maybe you assisted with the financial planning by making the tea and doing the typing for a team of accountants! Make sure that you say what you actually did. For example:

Analysing past financial performance to identify areas for future improvement, preparing budgets and creating financial models to ensure sound financial planning.

You may want to tailor the language and style of your CV to the culture of the organisation that you send it to. A new and dynamic company might be impressed if you described your current firm as aggressively competitive – a health service trust would probably conclude that you would not fit in with them.

Avoiding jargon

Most CVs need to include some 'technical' terms and abbreviations (for example, Brian's CV shown in Figure 3 talks about NVQs). However, you need to make sure that the recruiter can understand you. Remember that your CV may be screened by a human resources manager who is less familiar with technical terminology than a line manager would be. Avoid using jargon or acronyms unless you are certain they will be understood.

Being professional

Recruiters will not take you seriously unless your CV is businesslike and professional. Don't introduce jokes – few recruiters appreciate humour in a CV – and don't use gimmicks. Gimmicky CVs are occasionally successful for new graduates: at a senior level they send your application straight into the reject pile.

CREATING AN HONEST CV

Your CV should be made up of *positive* information about yourself. You will naturally present your achievements in the best possible light. There will also be information that does not help your case, which you want to leave out. You can usually omit details of failed exams, unsuccessful projects, jobs that lasted just a few weeks, and so on.

There is clearly a difference between putting yourself in a positive light and misleading the recruiter. Don't be economical with the truth on your CV:

◆ you may get caught out – many recruiters routinely check applicants' backgrounds

◆ if you talk yourself into a job that you can't do, you won't last long.

The background checking process

Employers are all too aware that some applicants falsify details of their experience, qualifications, reasons for leaving jobs and past salaries. In response, they are checking candidates' backgrounds more thoroughly than ever before.

Checks include:

+ taking up multiple references

+ asking new starters to provide original copies of their qualification certificates

+ checking with colleges and universities that the certificates provided are genuine

+ using specialist agencies to conduct pre-employment checks on candidates' education and past employment records.

Companies will not employ candidates who they discover have lied on their CV.

Pre-employment checks are particularly common in the teaching and caring professions, and in the defence and financial sectors. Their use is spreading to other industries and senior staff are among the first to be checked. **Avoid the temptation to embellish your CV.**

Question and answer session

'I was sacked from my last job after a disagreement with my boss. If I tell the truth on my CV how am I going to get another job?'

You don't need to put the reason why you left the job on your CV. You might also choose to use a skills-based CV format (see Chapter 4) to draw attention to your work experience and away from the fact that you left your last job without having another one to go to. However, interviewers are going to pick up on the fact that this happened and ask why. Prepare how you will answer questions in the most positive way possible and negotiate with your ex-employer over the reference that they are going to give you to ensure that they are not going to contradict what you say at interview. Many companies now only give standard references which state your last job title and the dates you were working at the organisation, and as a matter of policy do not divulge any further information.

'I have been promoted to a new role and am finding the demands too great. I want to apply for a job at a lower level but am concerned about what recruiters are going to think about this. Can I make my current job appear more junior than it is?'

Employers look for recruits who will find their job an exciting new challenge and are wary of taking on someone who appears to be overqualified. Giving the reason why you want to move down a gear – for example, that you want to spend more time with your children or found the responsibilities of your previous job too heavy – may also count against you. You do not have to emphasise how senior your current role is, as long as you do not mislead the recruiter. Take a positive stance as well – think through all the reasons why you want the new role and sell these to the employer in your covering letter and interview.

'I know that I can do this job, but I'm worried that the company will think that I'm too young. Can I hide my age?'

Your CV should stress the depth and breadth of your experience and your maturity of judgement and outlook. The fact that you have developed these qualities at a younger age than most should be a point in your favour. However, you don't need to put your date of birth in your CV (although the recruiter may wonder why you've omitted it) and you certainly don't need to state your age. Never state that you are a strong candidate *despite* your youth as this merely serves to draw attention to your age and might start to raise doubts in the employer's mind.

COMPLETING APPLICATION FORMS

If a company requires you to complete an application form, don't send a CV instead – it is unlikely that they will consider you further.

However, if you have already put together a CV, you have made the best possible preparation for completing an application form – you have identified your strengths and thought through how best to present them.

Getting your selling points on the form

The application form dictates the information that you must give but you still need to think through how to present this information for maximum impact.

Go through your list of 'selling points'. Decide how each of these can be included on the form and how the information in each section can be presented to your best advantage. Most forms have an 'Any Other Information' section, which can be a useful opportunity to include information on any of your strong points that are not naturally covered elsewhere.

♦ Be careful to follow any instructions given on the form – I know of one organisation that asked candidates to fill in their application form manually using black ink and automatically rejected anyone who used blue.

♦ Try to avoid cramming so much information into the space given that it becomes difficult for the reader to pick out the important points. If you really need more space, you can add an extra page or two, but it is best to avoid doing this as a reader scanning a pile of forms to select those of most interest may fail to read those pages.

MAKING THE MOST OF EMAIL

You will probably be sending out most of your CVs by email and the vast majority of medium and large companies have a sophisticated electronic system for handling your application. CVs are received by email, usually into a central account, passed by email to recruiting managers, and stored on a database which can be searched for relevant CVs when vacancies arise.

There is a number of ways in which you can work with the recruiter's IT systems in order to ensure that your CV gets noticed.

Sending your CV to the right place
Advertisements will always state how they would like CVs to be submitted. Where you are given a choice of email, post or fax you will usually find that email is not only the most convenient route for you, but also the recruiter's preferred method as well. Emailed CVs can usually be fed directly into the company's systems which prevents them from being lost or from failing to reach the right manager. Agencies and head-hunters have a strong preference for emailed CVs or online applications as this is the easiest form for them to use when distributing your information to recruiting companies.

Where you are sending a speculative CV, you will need to do some research into where your CV should be sent to. Most organisations have a set way in which they would like CVs submitted. In smaller organisations, it is often most appropriate to send your CV directly to the line manager concerned. In this situation a paper CV is more likely to catch the manager's attention (emails are easily deleted without being properly read) although you may wish to send an electronic version as backup, with your email referring to the fact you have already sent a paper copy.

Most sizeable organisations have a preferred route for speculative CVs to be submitted. They may wish candidates to apply online via their webpage, or they may ask for emails to be sent to a central address. This assists with the company's automated handling of applications. Find out from the organisation's webpage or HR department who your CV should be sent to. As the HR department will usually filter CVs before passing them on to line managers, you may also wish to send your CV to the head of the department which you wish to work for, with a note to say that you have also applied to the company via their preferred route.

Making sure your CV is readable
By the time your CV has been automatically processed by the recruiter, it may look very different from the document you saw on your screen.

◆ Always attach your CV as an electronic document – don't send a scanned copy. Scanned documents are harder to read and databases often have difficulty in recording the information.

◆ Don't simply cut and paste your CV into the body of your email as the formatting will be lost. While the formatting is often lost in the course of your CV being processed, you should give your CV the opportunity to be seen in its most professional form.

◆ Don't password protect your attachment.

♦ Follow any instructions given in an advertisement for quoting reference numbers in your email; these are often used to automatically sort applications.

♦ If you are applying for a specific post, put the title in the header of the CV.

♦ Keep the formatting in your CV simple. Spacing is often altered dramatically when a CV is entered onto an organisation's database and features such as bold and underline are lost. Make sure that your CV will be understandable even after the recruiter has processed it.

♦ Don't attach a covering letter as a separate document as it is likely to become detached from the CV itself in the course of processing. Include introductory information in the body of the email and remember that this too may get detached from the CV.

Catching the attention of search engines
Many large companies keep electronic copies of the CVs that they receive on a central database. When a vacancy arises, the CVs on the database are searched to see if they contain relevant keywords. Make sure your CV contains the words or phrases which a recruiter is likely to search for. The most likely examples of these are:

♦ Generally recognised job titles, such as Solicitor, Mechanical Engineer or PR Manager. If your company has given your role an unusual title, you may wish to change it on your CV, although you will need to make it clear to the recruiter that you have done this before they take up a reference from your employer.

- Generally recognised key skills and qualifications, e.g. 'Offshore Survival Certificate' or 'project management'.

- The names of computer languages, software packages and operating systems.

- Words which highlight the technology and experience relevant to roles in your profession or sector, for example 'polyethylene', 'Saudi Arabia' and 'Prince II'.

CHECKLIST

- Is your CV an appropriate length?

- Have you eliminated all irrelevant information?

- Is the most relevant information at the top of your CV?

- Have you provided supporting evidence for all the claims you have made?

- Have you sold your achievements using positive language?

- Would your CV stand up to a rigorous pre-employment check?

POINTS TO CONSIDER

1. Which of your achievements would make the most powerful first impression on a recruiter?

2. Pick three words or phrases which most accurately convey the professional image that you want to convey to the recruiter (for example, *meticulous, accurate, analytical;* or *creative, strategic thinker, business acumen*). Have you included these in your CV?

3. Would your search for work be helped if you prepared a version of your CV for the internet?

(4)

Your Career and Achievements

The Career and Achievements section is the most important part
of a senior CV. Junior staff can demonstrate their potential
through their educational achievements and hobbies; a manager or
professional has to show a record of achievement within their
chosen field. Details of your education and outside interests can
add weight to your CV, but it is the Career and Achievements
section that proves to the recruiter that you have the skills to
succeed in the job on offer.

CHOOSING AN APPROPRIATE FORMAT

There are two main ways to present your career and achievements:

- the time-based CV
- the skills-based CV.

Each is suitable in different circumstances.

The time-based CV

The time-based CV is the traditional style of CV. It gives details of
each post that you have held, starting with the most recent and
working backwards through time. This is the most common type of
CV and is the format preferred by most employers. It emphasises
progression through a number of posts over time. It is a useful
format to use where:

◆ you have worked for a relatively small number of employers
◆ your employment history is one of progression in a career
◆ you are currently in work
◆ you are applying for a job in the same field that you are currently working in
◆ you have worked for prestigious employers
◆ you are applying for a job in a relatively traditional field or organisation.

Case study – Sue's CV

Sue has held only four jobs to date, and can show a history of uncomplicated career progression. A time-based CV is therefore the logical choice for her (see Figure 4).

The skills-based CV

This style of CV is based on the skills and knowledge that you are offering the recruiter rather than the posts that you have held. Because it emphasises your abilities and your achievements, it is perhaps a more logical way of selling yourself to an employer. It is also more suitable for presenting a modern career where the individual builds up a portfolio of skills by moving through a series of varied jobs. Despite this, many recruiters want their candidates to show a career of orderly upward progress. They suspect that skills-based CVs are used to hide patchy work histories and they therefore prefer the traditional time-based CV. However, the skills-based CV is a useful format to use where:

◆ you have worked for a large number of employers

◆ you have worked in a number of different fields or careers

◆ you have had a career break or a number of spells of unemployment

SUSAN BROWN
24 Mounds Road, Walton, Hampshire PT29 3QE
Home Telephone: 00000 111 2222
Mobile: 11111 222 3333
email: sb7006@ameritech.com

PROFILE

A professional Facilities Manager with eleven years' experience of managing projects, staff, budgets and contracts to ensure the smooth running of office facilities. Associate of the Royal Institution of Chartered Surveyors.

CAREER AND ACHIEVEMENTS

DATACO HEAD OFFICE, Portsea, Hants

Maintenance Manager (June XX – Present)
Managing the maintenance function for a prestigious head office accommodating 300 staff and five regional offices accommodating a total of 500 staff. Achievements include:

◆ Preparing the head office for occupation following Dataco's purchase of the site, including management of a major refurbishment of the ground floor within budget and to a tight deadline.
◆ Preparing and controlling the maintenance budget. Careful control has resulted in costs being below median in every year that benchmarking against similar companies has been undertaken.
◆ Managing all maintenance contracts through the complete process of requirements analysis, tender process, negotiation, development of Service Level Agreements and ongoing management.
◆ Supervising up to twenty maintenance contractors on site.

COLEFAX FACILITIES MANAGEMENT

Project Manager (Feb XX – June XX)
Assistant Project Manager (Sept XX – Feb XX)
Management of increasingly large contracts including the maintenance contracts for DrugStore's Harport Regional Office, and Computerworld's Westport site. Ensuring all maintenance and minor works completed to clients' satisfaction; management of refurbishment projects; developing, agreeing and implementing Service Level Agreements; and developing cost control procedures.

Graduate Trainee (June XX – Sept XX)
Training in all aspects of facilities management.

EDUCATION

BSc (Hons) 2:2 Building Surveying Yorkshire University
Sept XX – June XX
3 A levels North Hill School, London Sept XX – June XX

ADDITIONAL INFORMATION

◆ Date of birth XX/XX/XX
◆ Full, clean driving licence
◆ Health – excellent
◆ References available on request
◆ Interests – voluntary work organising outings for disabled children with the Sunshine Trust.

Fig. 4. Sue's time-based CV.

◆ you are not currently in work

◆ you have developed valuable skills in unpaid work

◆ you are applying for a job demanding skills that you possess, but have not used in recent posts

◆ you are changing career, and want to emphasise your transferable skills rather than the fact that you gained them in an environment different from the one you now want to enter – this is particularly useful for ex-armed forces personnel.

Case study – Steve's CV

Steve has spent the last seven years working as a contractor. He has developed a great portfolio of experience but all in relatively short-term contracts. If he was to compile a traditional time-based CV:

◆ No recruiter could spare the time to read through the long list of all the projects he has worked on.

◆ The fact that he sometimes works on more than one project at a time would be confusing.

◆ His experience as a systems analyst would be emphasised, because most of his work has been in this area. Steve wants to move away from systems analyst roles into project management and he therefore needs to draw attention to his project management skills.

For these reasons, Steve decides to present his career and achievements section in a skills-based format (see Figure 5). He divides this information into three sections:

Steven Black
2 Heaton Road, Northmoor, South Yorkshire SY34 9LB
Tel/Fax: 00000 111222   Mobile: 1111 666666
E-mail sb@internet.co.uk

PROFILE

An experienced information technology Project Manager and Chartered Engineer. Manages the full lifecycle from requirements specification to implementation. Ensures that optimum business solutions are delivered to meet customer requirements and within budget.

KEY SKILLS

Project Manager

Implementing projects with a value of up to £1 million to meet clients' time, budget and quality standards. Recent projects have included:

◆ Redeveloping a customer information database to a tight deadline for the Clothesco mail order company. Migrating the records of 20,000 customers from an ITCO mainframe to a Megatech platform; improving data quality control methods (e.g. error reporting and change control) to improve accuracy of records and reduce customer complaints. Managing system testing, verification and acceptance of the system.

◆ Analysing the engineering information requirements of North Sea Engineering plc. Designing and implementing a secure company intranet system to improve the speed of data access, reduce paperwork and ensure that data is up to date. Producing supporting documentation, managing the training of 100 staff at all levels of the organisation in the new system, ensuring a smooth handover to the operational team, and providing ongoing support.

◆ Implementing an Ameritech-based payroll system for 5,000 staff at Supercorp UK.

Business Systems Analyst

Analysing complex business systems, working closely with clients to ensure a detailed understanding of their needs, and designing a range of solutions. Projects have included:

◆ Analysing and designing a stock control information system for 50 retail outlets in the Cheapprice Shops Group, resulting in a 10% reduction in stock holding costs and faster delivery of merchandise. Finding solutions to conflicting needs of different departments.

Fig. 5. Steve's skills-based CV.

- Analysing complex business processes and designing business solutions for a wide variety of firms including Pharmco, Supra Cars, Megabank, Tomorrow Group and DrugStore.

INFORMATION TECHNOLOGY

Environments
Intranet, WAN, ITCO Mainframe, Megatech (VDX, ODP) Tech 6.1 Megasoft Networking, Opsys 04, Opsys 03, Ameritech.

Programming languages
ITCO LANGSYS, A++ Babel, Intlang.

Software
Microsoft Office, Microsoft Project.

Internet
Voyager, Outlook, Intlang.

CAREER SUMMARY

Contract work for a wide variety of blue-chip companies in the financial services, retail, mail order, manufacturing and engineering sectors. June XX – Present

Project Manager	Circo Systems	Feb XX – June XX
Team Leader	Megacomp	Mar XX – Feb XX
Senior Systems Analyst	Megacomp	Nov XX – Mar XX
Computer Programmer/ Analyst	World Computer plc	Feb XX – Nov XX
Graduate Trainee	World Computer plc	Sept XX – Feb XX

EDUCATION

BSc (Hons) Electrical & Electronic Engineering 2:1, Southcoast University XX – XX
3 A levels, 7 O levels, Selby School, Portchester XX – XX

INTERESTS

I enjoy playing golf and cricket and am currently a member of the Clothesco cricket team.

ADDITIONAL INFORMATION

- Full, clean driving licence
- DOB – XX/XX/XX
- Health – excellent
- References available on request

Fig. 5. (contd).

◆ Key Skills.

◆ Information Technology – this is a separate section because Steve needs to list all the systems and packages that he is familiar with.

◆ Career Summary – giving information on his employment history. He has summarised the years that he has spent working as a contractor, as the recruiter neither needs nor wants to know details of every single company that he has worked for during this time.

Experiment to see which style of CV suits you best. In addition to the time-based CV that Brian created, which is shown in Figure 3, he also put together a skills-based one to apply for the post at Zipco – see Figure 6.

THE TIME-BASED CV

The time-based CV shows your career history, starting with your most recent job and moving back in reverse chronological order through posts that you held previously.

Your current or last post will usually be the one of most interest to the recruiter and will therefore be given the most space and emphasis. Occasionally, you may want to give more emphasis to a previous post which is more relevant to the one that you are applying for. If you are in this situation, consider whether the skills-based CV format would be more appropriate. Normally, you will give less and less detail on posts as you work backwards through time, and only a broad outline will be given on roles that you held more than fifteen years ago. This is because:

BRIAN WHITE
87 Chambers Walk, Crawton, Surrey, GT7 9XQ
Telephone: 01234-567890 (Home) 01234-876543 (Mobile)
email: bw@internet.co.uk

Profile
An experienced Training Manager with a wide range of experience in the engineering industry. An expert in providing training and development solutions to meet business needs.

Key Skills

Training and Development
◆ Providing a full training and development support service to the British Engineering Aeronautical Division (BEAeD), an operation employing 600 people in the manufacture of sophisticated electronic control systems. Working with the management team to analyse the company's training and development needs and implement effective solutions.

◆ Purchasing IT; management & interpersonal skills; health & safety; and technical skills training courses. Achieving a 30% saving in the BEAeD Training and Development budget through effective targeting of training courses and outsourcing IT skills training through competitive tender.

◆ Designing and delivering management, interpersonal skills, and induction courses to staff at all levels within a number of British Engineering divisions.

Management Development
◆ Introducing a Personal Development Programme for managers and selected high-potential British Engineering employees in association with Oak Hall Consultants. 70% of participants' managers rated this programme 'excellent' or 'very good' at improving the skills of their people.

◆ Managing the BEAeD succession planning, management development, graduate training and Modern Apprenticeship programmes to ensure that key roles are filled by highly competent and motivated employees.

Technical Skills Training
◆ Meeting the BEAeD's need to improve the technical skills of manufacturing staff with the introduction of training to NVQ standards. This has contributed to a 12% fall in the number of units rejected during quality inspection.

Fig. 6. Brian's skills-based CV.

- Setting up and supervising apprenticeship and modern apprenticeship training schemes.

Generalist HR Management
- Devising and implementing HR strategies to support the BEAeD in meeting its business aims of quality improvement and the introduction of new manufacturing processes. Providing compensation & benefits, industrial relations, recruitment, database & payroll management and personnel administration services.
- Managing industrial relations, moving from a culture of conflict towards more effective working relationships.

Career Summary

British Engineering (Aeronautical Division) Crawton, Surrey
- Human Resources Manager (March XX – Present)
- Training Manager (Feb XX – Feb XX)

British Engineering Motor Components Ltd Petersham, Cambs
- Personnel Manager (July XX – Feb XX)

Motor Components, Light Engineering and Heavy Engineering divisions of British Engineering (Sept XX – Feb XX)
- A variety of training and personnel roles

Between February XXXX and September XXXX I built up experience in a variety of clerical jobs in Coshall, Cheshire.

Interests

I am a keen runner and cyclist. I enjoy taking part in fun runs and charity cycle rides.

Additional Information

- Willing to relocate within the UK and travel worldwide
- Clean, full driving licence
- Health – excellent
- References available on request

Fig. 6. (contd).

- you want to keep your CV to a readable length
- you want the reader to concentrate on your highest-profile post, most recent achievements and up-to-date skills.

Many people draw up a CV at the start of their career, and simply add to it as they go along. This can lead to an unwieldy document full of irrelevant information. If your CV is like this, put it to one side. Start again with a blank piece of paper and the question 'What does the recruiter need to know about my career to date?'

The golden rule when writing a CV is never to leave unexplained gaps in your career history. A suspicious recruiter many wonder whether you were in prison or doing something that you want to hide during that time. If – like an increasing number of job applicants – you were a homemaker, travelling or unemployed for a period, put this information in the correct place in your history.

What to include
For each position that you have held, you should include:

The name of the company
Unless your employer is well known, a short description of the business may help the reader (for example – 'Smith and Jones Ltd are the largest manufacturer of quality widgets in the UK'). You may also want to state where the organisation is or was located. This does not have to be the full address, especially for jobs that you held in the past.

The position(s) that you held
These should be listed in reverse chronological order. If you never had a job title, or your title was confusing or misleading in some

way, choose an appropriate name that accurately and honestly reflects what you did. For example, your firm might have called you an 'operations support analyst', but it is going to give the reader a much clearer picture of what your role was if you tell them that you were a market researcher.

The dates that you worked
Add the dates that you worked for the company or held each post. If you are still in a job, show this as, for example, 'June 2003 – Present' or otherwise your CV will quickly become out of date. You can put this in even if you know that your job is about to come to an end. For your recent career history, the recruiter will want to know the months that you started and finished in a job as well as the years.

What you achieved
This is the core of your CV. If you could only tell the employer one thing about yourself, this would be it. Note that the focus should be on achievements rather than duties. Junior CVs focus on the duties of the post. Senior ones may detail the responsibilities held, but the emphasis must be on what you achieved in the role. Your key selling points should come over clearly in this section.

Exercise 1
Think about each of the last three posts that you have held. What would a recruiter see as your most important achievements during your time in that post?

Now rank the achievements in each post within order of importance to select which ones you are going to put on your CV.

To ensure that the reader focuses on the most important points, you should describe a maximum of six achievements in your most recent post, and give less detail about previous jobs.

Exercise 2

For each of the achievements that you wrote down in Exercise 1, ask yourself:

◆ What are the most important points about this achievement that the recruiter needs to know?

◆ Does this achievement reflect my key selling points?

Then describe each achievement in one or two sentences for your CV.

Question and answer session

'I am a general practitioner. I can see how a manager within a business might be able to concentrate on their achievements – he or she is employed to complete projects successfully and hit targets. As a doctor, my measure of success is the quality of care that I provide to my patients. How should I present this part of my CV?'

As a professional, the accent is on your skills, knowledge and competence. The key points listed under each post that you have held could concentrate on describing:

◆ The nature of the work that you did, showing the challenges that you faced and the skills that you have therefore developed. For example:
Managing a caseload of 2,200 patients in a deprived inner-city area. Approximately 60% of patients are from ethnic minorities and a

*significant proportion do not speak English. Sensitivity to patients'
culture and religion is an important part of meeting their needs.*

◆ Areas of specialist knowledge, interest and skill that you have
gained during your time in the post. For example:
*Developing an understanding of the needs of the elderly in my
work as a GP: supporting a home for 50 active senior citizens, 100
people living in warden-controlled sheltered housing and three
homes for frail elderly people.*

◆ Finally, you may have contributed to meeting targets and
completing projects. For example:
*Set up an asthma clinic which to date has helped 200 patients
manage their condition.*
*As manager of the practice finances, I reduced running expenses
by 10% over three years.*
*Brought about a 50% increase in the numbers of women going for
cervical smears by working with practice and community nurses to
educate patients on the need for regular health checks.*

What to leave out

Don't give the reasons why you left each job that you have held
unless you are specifically asked to by the recruiter. If you left for
a post with better prospects and more responsibility it should be
obvious from your description of that next job. Any other reason
may reflect badly on you. Never admit on your CV to having left
a company because, for example, you couldn't get on with your
boss.

Laying out the information

The details of your career and achievements must be clear and
easy to read. The best format for laying out your information on
each post is usually:

Job title   *Name of company*   *Dates post held*

What you did in the job will probably be more important than the company in which you did it, so the job title is placed to the left where it will be the first thing that the reader sees. If the company you worked for was very prestigious, you can reverse these two items. The start and finish dates for each job are of lesser importance, and therefore appear on the right of the page.

Question and answer session

'I have had an unusual career pattern. After doing a number of different jobs, I went back to college as a mature student and changed career. How do I present this information so that the recruiter doesn't think I'm a job hopper who can't stick to one thing for long?'

As the labour market changes, fewer and fewer people enjoy a traditional career of unbroken progress in one specialism. CVs often show:

- career breaks to pursue full-time education or look after children
- career changes
- periods of unemployment
- working for a wide variety of employers.

Most employers are now used to this. Many appreciate the breadth of perspective and skills that this kind of career can offer. Try to show a logical pattern behind your career history with each move developing your skills and abilities further and an underlying purpose or area of expertise. It could be that your career has been one of caring for children, first as a nurse and then as a teacher; or managing teams, first in the armed forces

and then in industry. It also helps if you can show a positive
reason for career changes – perhaps because in your first career
you were able to identify an area of strength that you wanted to
build on. If you have spent some time outside of paid work, this
needs to be shown on your CV to avoid leaving a suspicious-
looking gap, for example:

Homemaker Sept XX – Mar XX
or
Job hunting following redundancy July XX – Sept XX

*'I have spent fifteen years with one company. Won't new employers
think I'm stuck in my ways?'*

If you have had many years of experience with one employer, you
will need to show that you have grown, progressed and gained a
breadth of experience within that organisation. If you have held a
number of posts there, you may want to emphasise this fact by
dividing the information that you give on your time with that
organisation into a number of subsections (see Figure 7).

*'I ran my own business for several years, but did not make enough
money to make it viable in the long term. How do I present this
information on a CV?'*

Identify and sell your achievements as you would if you had been
employed. Running your own business demonstrates that you have
developed:

◆ self-discipline and motivation
◆ commercial acumen
◆ a broad understanding of how business works

Senior Research Chemist, Europlastics, Beaconsfield June XX –
Sept XX
- xxxxxxxxxxxxxxxxxxxxxxxxxxxxxx
- xxxxxxxxxxxxxxxxxxxxxxxxxxxxxxxxxxxxxxxxxxxxxxxxx
- xxxxxxxxxxxxxxxxxxxxxxxxxxxxxxxxxxxxxxxxxxxxx
- xxxxxxxxxxxxxxxxxxxxx
- xxxxxxxxxxxxxxxxxxxxxxxxxxxxxxxx

Research Chemist, Europlastics, Dortmund, Germany
August XX – June XX
- xxxxxxxxxxxxxxxxxxxxxxxxxxxxxxxxxxxxxxxx
- xxxxxxxxxxxxxxxxxxxxxxx
- xxxxxxxxxxxxxxxxxxxxxxxxxxx

**Research Scientist, Mouldings UK (a member of the Europlastics
group), Edinburgh** May XX – August XX
- xxxxxxxxxxxxxxxxxxxxxxx
- xxxxxxxxxxxxxxxxxxxxxxxxxxx

Graduate Trainee, Europlastics, Edinburgh
June XX – May XX
- xxxxxxxxxxxxxxxxxxxxxxxxxxx

Fig. 7. The one-company career.

- an entrepreneurial perspective, which is of great worth to many
  organisations.

If you were recently self-employed, you might want to put in a
positive reason for your wish to switch to employment to reassure
the employer that you will be happy working for someone else.

*'I've been on maternity leave twice. How do I present this on my
CV?'*

If you took a few months off and then returned to work with the
same firm, your CV doesn't need to say that you were on
maternity leave. The same principle applies if you have been on

long-term sick leave. It isn't a selling point with employers, so leave it out. If you resigned from your job and took a longer break, treat it as you would a career break (see above).

THE SKILLS-BASED CV

A skills-based CV enables you to put an emphasis firmly on what you can do, rather than when you last did it or when you learnt to do it. It is organised around your most relevant and marketable skills. For example, someone looking for a post managing a mechanic's workshop might show the following on their CV:

Workshop manager
- control and inspection of workshop equipment
- purchasing and control of all workshop spare parts
- control of all workshop documentation.

Team leader
- managing teams of up to twenty mechanics, technicians and office staff
- staff recruitment
- running apprenticeship and Modern Apprenticeship training schemes, successfully training over 30 young people during my career
- organising rotas for 24-hour emergency breakdown cover.

Engineer
- extensive experience of the repair, maintenance and testing of vehicles of all kinds, including light, commercial and heavy vehicles and petrol and diesel engines.

Exercise 1

Look at your key selling points. Think through the last ten years of your career. Then ask yourself the question:

◆ What are my most marketable skills?

Once you have compiled a list, rank them in order of importance. To ensure that the recruiter focuses on the most relevant points, pick no more than six of your most important skills for your CV. These will form the subheadings of your Career and Achievements section.

Exercise 2

For each skill heading that you created in Exercise 1, ask the questions:

◆ How can I prove that I have this skill?
◆ What are my most important achievements in this area?

Rank the points within each section in order of importance. To maintain focus, there should be a maximum of six points under each heading with fewer points shown under the headings lower down the list.

Choosing your section headings

While it is tempting to copy the section headings from someone else's CV, this will lead you into difficulties later on as you try to fit your information into unsuitable categories. The skills sections that you choose should reflect your own personal selling points and your unique abilities and career history.

Voluntary work

It may be appropriate to list some skills that you developed outside regular employment. For example, you may have developed your team-building skills in the Territorial Army or your flair for organising events in part-time voluntary work. These 'selling points' can be fitted into your skill groupings in the same way as those gained working for an employer. However, the main focus of your CV must be on your achievements in regular employment.

Question and answer session

'I have spent five years on a career break looking after my young children. I am now looking to re-enter employment as an engineer. While I have been on career break, I have managed a household budget, developed interpersonal skills coping with fractious toddlers, and learned how to do six things at once! Can I include these skills on my CV?'

Not if you are looking for a job at a senior level. Unfortunately, listing skills that you have acquired as a homemaker detracts from your professional image. It also emphasises the fact that you have not been in paid employment for a number of years. You can, however, include information on any freelance or voluntary work that you have done during this time – for example, helping to run a playgroup, or work with a parent–teacher association.

Listing your past employers

A description of your skills should always be followed by a summary of your career. Ideally, this should be a list of each of your past employers in reverse chronological order, with the posts that you held at each and relevant dates. However, if you have held down a great number of jobs, then this may not be practical – and you may not remember details of the jobs you were doing 30 years ago! If this is the case, select a list of your major employers – including, of course, the most prestigious and those with the closest links to the recruiting company or industry.

SUMMARIES

There will be situations in which it is appropriate to summarise a period of your career rather than give details of every post that you held during that time.

The long career

Your CV should concentrate on posts that you have held in recent years. Much less information will need to be given on earlier jobs, particularly those you worked in over fifteen years ago.

Those nearer the end of their working lives might want to show details of whole decades in summary form – for example:

Self-employed trader – 1965–1975
Graduated from trading on market stalls in the Cardiff area to owning and managing a ladies' fashions shop in Pontypridd.

Or:

Gained experience of retailing in a number of junior positions – 1960–1970.

This prevents valuable space on your CV being taken up with out-of-date information and means the reader focuses on the information on your more recent and relevant career history. Drawing attention away from jobs that you did many years ago is particularly useful if you are concerned that you may be discriminated against on the grounds of your age. It is also useful if you have had a change of career or have risen to the top from humble beginnings. The managing director of a retail conglomerate will not wish to go into details of the years he or she spent stacking shelves and working on the tills.

The career change

If you have changed career, you will not want to give detailed
information on the jobs that you did in your first specialism. You
will, however, want to sell the transferable skills that you
developed. For example, a businesswoman who originally trained
as a nurse might wish to summarise this period as follows:

Registered General Nurse 1981–1992
Gaining full professional qualifications at St Cedric's Hospital,
London. Developing my career working in a variety of hospitals,
reaching the position of Sister in charge of the Accident and
Emergency ward and a team of ten nurses. This experience has
given me a high level of interpersonal skills and the ability to
manage a team working under extreme pressure.

Short-term jobs

Many job hunters have spent a period of their career working in a
number of short-term jobs. This could be for any of the following
reasons:

◆ career development through temporary or contract work
◆ filling in while looking for a permanent post
◆ time out travelling
◆ moving around while following a spouse's career.

This may be time during which you developed very valuable skills,
but you should not clutter up your CV with the details of each
temporary post. The period can be summarised as in the following
examples:

Temporary jobs   *XXXX – XXXX*
Temporary secretarial, clerical and bar work while travelling around Australia and New Zealand.

Or

Contract Site Manager   *XXXX – XXXX*
Managing teams of builders constructing homes and offices around the UK and Germany. Major employers included:

- *Millar Construction plc*
- *Morgan Homes*
- *A. G. Arthur and Sons*
- *Lloyd and Logan Construction*
- *Jabusch-Wiemer Gmbh.*

CHECKLIST

- Have you given most room on your CV to your most recent and relevant experience?

- Have you made sure that there are no gaps in your employment history?

- Have you included all the information that the recruiter will want to know about your previous employers?

- Are you confident that you have not included too much information?

- Have you focused on your achievements, rather than your duties?

- If you are using a skills-based CV format, is the information on your career organised under appropriate headings?

POINTS TO CONSIDER

1. Would a time-based or a skills-based CV be the most appropriate way of presenting your career? Why?

2. What are your three main achievements in your career to date? Are these clearly presented on your CV?

3. Would it be helpful if your CV summarised a period of your career?

5

The Rest of Your CV

The Career and Achievements section is the core of your CV and should make up the largest part of the document. You will, of course, need to add your contact details. You have some flexibility in choosing what else to add to your CV, basing your decision on what will help to sell you to the recruiter. You should almost certainly include at least one of the following:

◆ details of your education, training and qualifications

◆ an eye-catching summary of what you have to offer the recruiter

◆ details of your involvement with relevant professional bodies

◆ information on your hobbies and interests to give a fuller picture of what you are like as a person

◆ details of additional skills that you can offer – for example, languages or IT skills.

At the beginning of your career, you may have given much more weight to these elements of your CV. A recent graduate, for example, usually has little to show in the way of career achievement and therefore concentrates on selling the potential demonstrated in their academic successes, leadership of sports teams, and so on. After five years in a career the emphasis should have shifted to focus on proof that you have succeeded in your career (and by implication will succeed in the future).

MAKING A GOOD START
Title
Don't start your CV with the title CURRICULUM VITAE. Start instead with your name at the top in bold capitals. This is a better use of the space and helps the recruiter find your CV from amongst a pile of others.

Use the name by which you are generally known rather than your full legal name. The recruiter just needs to know what to call you, not what appears on your birth certificate. If everyone calls you David Perkins it simply causes confusion if you give your name as Charles David Arthur Perkins. However, avoid nicknames ('Dave Perkins') as this looks less professional.

Contact details
Add your contact details under your name. As a minimum, you should give your:

◆ full home address including postcode

◆ home telephone number including dialling code (if possible, also include a mobile number, and add a note to let the recruiter know which number is which).

You may also want to add your:

◆ work number
◆ email address.

Only give contact details which will be genuinely useful. Do you check your email daily or just occasionally? If the recruiter calls you on your mobile number, will you be able to speak to him or her or will you be in a business meeting with your current employer?

If you are based abroad, put your contact details at the end of your CV. This means that the employer reads what you have to offer before they are confronted with the information that arranging an interview with you will take extra effort. Email addresses are useful when contacting expatriates – but make sure you check your mailbox every day!

CREATING AN ATTENTION-GRABBING SUMMARY

A summary at the top of the page showing what you have to offer the recruiter may grab their attention and make them read more. For example:

Production manager with ten years' experience in managing the manufacture of electrical and electronic components. Excellent track record of improving quality standards while reducing overheads in unionised environments.

This draws maximum attention to your key selling points. If they match the recruiter's needs, you have given them a good reason to look through the rest of your CV. For this reason, summaries are particularly useful on speculative applications. However, the summary must closely fit the position on offer. If you are prepared to consider a wide range of career options, leave this section out when making speculative applications or sending a CV to an agency (which may consider you for jobs other than the one that you have applied for).

Preparing a summary

Summaries can give a punchy and positive précis of your CV and hook the reader's attention, but all too often they are weak, waffling or grandiose. If you decide to include a summary in your CV, start with a positive statement of what you are – an 'experienced optician' or a 'senior marine engineer', for example – and follow this with a brief statement of your most marketable qualities. You should always aim to keep this down to three sentences and avoid use of the words 'I' or 'we': as you are selling your best points, you can otherwise appear very egotistical.

Question and answer session
'I've heard that many recruiters don't like summaries. Why is this?'

Too many summaries are just empty hype. Statements such as 'Dynamic and visionary sales executive with excellent interpersonal skills and a track record of success in challenging environments' tell the reader very little and look false. By all means sell your strong points, but make them factual. Perhaps this summary could be rewritten as 'Sales executive with ten years' experience in cosmetics and beauty care products. Track record of building winning teams and expanding market share in Europe and Asia.' Back up each statement you make in the summary with evidence in another part of your CV, and if you can't back up a point with evidence, leave it out.

EDUCATION AND TRAINING

The summary of your educational background should come after the details of your employment, unless you have deeply impressive achievements and are applying for a job in a field where academic excellence is important.

Your professional qualification

From the recruiter's point of view your most important academic achievement is your professional qualification. Either the summary at the top of your CV or your Education and Training section should tell the recruiter that you are a fully qualified professional – for example, that you are a State Registered Nurse or Chartered Engineer. The most important part of your Education and Training section will be the details of your professional training, demonstrating that you have passed all the necessary examinations. Avoid any ambiguity. For example, stating that you 'studied for electrical engineering BTEC HNC examinations' could mean that you took the course but did not pass the exams.

How much should you say?

The amount of space you should devote to your education and training depends on:

♦ the importance that qualifications will have in deciding whether you get the job

♦ how recent your qualifications are.

When you were a graduate or school-leaver, this will have been the largest section on your CV. Now you are well established in your career, your CV should be focused on your achievements at work, and you need to start pruning the information on your education.

What to leave out

Omit the details of old or irrelevant qualifications. Senior and professional CVs should not include information on any of the following:

- dates and grades of GCSEs, O levels, etc.
- schools attended before the age of eleven
- courses that you failed or were unable to finish
- qualifications irrelevant to your present career; for example, your secretarial training if you are now a manager.

If you cannot omit the last two without leaving an unexplained gap in your career history, keep the details as brief as possible.

What to summarise

Other information should be given in summary form. If you are a graduate you should not include the full details of your A levels, Highers, HNC or similar qualifications. A simple statement that you got 3 A levels is often enough information for the recruiter – they do not need to know subjects, grades and the dates that you took the examinations. Older candidates may go further and decide that it is irrelevant to put in any details of their secondary schooling. If you have many years of experience but few formal qualifications, then you may decide that a section on your education is irrelevant.

If you have more than three years' work experience since graduation, the full details of your degree course are no longer relevant. Leave out details of the modules taken and the interim grades given – all the recruiter will be interested in is the title and class of your degree and the date it was awarded. The exception will be where you studied for a module relevant to the post you are applying for. For example, if you are applying for a post in Spain, you might want to highlight the fact that your business degree included courses in Spanish and international business.

Question and answer session

'I graduated with a first from a very prestigious university twenty-five years ago with a number of prizes for my work. My career is in marketing. I know that this is not a field where academic achievement is of paramount importance, but shouldn't my CV give my education top billing to impress recruiters?'

Your academic achievements are impressive. However, if you devote a lot of space to them, your CV draws attention to what you were doing twenty-five years ago – and the recruiter is much more interested in what you have to offer *now*. It also gives the impression that you hark back to past glories and have achieved nothing to match them since. Keep the entry on your university career brief – a recruiter will still be impressed to see that you got a first.

School and college education

Give the details of your school and college education, listing:

◆ your schools/colleges
◆ the dates you attended them
◆ the qualifications that you gained.

For example:

Business Studies with German BSc (Hons) 2:2
Bridgethorpe University   *XXXX – XXXX*

HNC in Business Studies (pass)
1 A level
Spelthorpe Technical College   *XXXX – XXXX*

1 A level
Sedgewick Secondary School, Windlesham   *XXXX – XXXX*

This layout shows the course first, which draws the reader's attention to the qualification that you gained rather than where and when you studied. However, if you want to draw attention to your prestigious university and away from a less relevant degree, you would lay this section out as follows:

Oxbridge University
Anthropology BA (Hons) 2:2   *XXXX – XXXX*

If you obtained your qualifications abroad, you may need to help the reader to understand the level of your qualifications. For example, a UK employer may not quite understand what a baccalaureate is or what a GPA of 3.8 represents. Provide a few brief words of explanation.

Work-related short courses
This is a section that is important in a junior CV but can often be omitted from a senior one. You should only give details of work-related short courses if this information is going to make you stand out in the eyes of the recruiter because, for example, you:

- have been trained in a specific technical skill
- keep up to date in your field
- have developed your managerial or interpersonal skills.

Details of work-related short courses are most useful if you are applying for work in an area where you need a licence or safety permit to do certain jobs. For example, an engineer applying for a job working offshore will have an advantage if he or she already has the relevant safety certificates and can therefore start immediately. This is particularly important for contractors as employers will be unwilling to pay for (or wait for) training. However, it is usually better to be able to show that you have developed particular skills through what you have achieved in your job. For example, it is better to give details of negotiations that you have successfully concluded than of the negotiation skills course that you attended.

If you have undertaken further education (for example, an MBA or training towards your professional qualifications) you should put the details of this into the section on your Education and Training.

What to avoid
There is a number of pitfalls that you should be aware of if you do decide to include details of the short courses you have taken:

◆ If you have been given training in a particular area of managerial or interpersonal skills, a recruiter may suspect that this is because you are naturally weak in this area. For example, they may wonder if you have taken an assertiveness course because you are too timid, or that you have undergone time management training because you are poor at organising yourself.

◆ If you list a large number of courses, you give the impression that you spend a disproportionate amount of time (and company money) training.

◆ Don't include details of course providers and dates of your courses unless this adds useful information – for example, showing that the safety certificate that you gained is still valid.

◆ Don't waste space with details of irrelevant courses.

Studying as a hobby

If you have good academic and work-related qualifications but have studied an unrelated subject as a hobby, put the details in your Hobbies and Interests section. This avoids distracting the reader's attention from your relevant qualifications.

Exam certificates

Don't include copies of your exam certificates with your application unless you are specifically asked to. Most employers will only want to see evidence of your qualifications later in the recruitment process.

MEMBERSHIPS OF PROFESSIONAL ASSOCIATIONS

Membership of a professional association shows that you are serious about your career. Give details of your affiliation to the association(s) that you are a member of and include details of any honorary posts that you have held. If these details come to more than a line or two, organise the information into a section on its own. For example:

Member of the Society of Pipeline Engineers
◆ *London Section Chairperson XXXX – XXXX*
◆ *Member of National Award Committee XXXX*

Member of the Royal Society of Industrial Engineers

HOBBIES AND INTERESTS

It is not always appropriate to add this section to a senior CV. An inexperienced new graduate's hobbies may give valuable information on the individual's leadership potential or ability to work in a team. At a senior level you will be expected to show that you have these qualities through your achievements in your job, with outside interests being used as additional backup only.

How information on your interests can be helpful

Information on your outside interests may help you in the following ways:

◆ It helps the recruiter to build up a fuller picture of what you are like as a person. Your interests give further indications as to whether you are a teamworker, organised, creative, etc. You may also, quite simply, come across as a more interesting person.

◆ Your interests may give extra evidence that you have particular aptitudes and skills; for example, a flair for organising events or working with people.

◆ Success in outside interests adds weight to the picture you are building of yourself as an achiever.

◆ Outside interests show that you are able to relax and recuperate at the end of a stressful day.

◆ Sporting interests suggest that you are fit and healthy.

◆ Involvement in the community (for example, in local politics or the Round Table) may indicate that you have a useful network of contacts and/or that you could help generate good local PR for the company.

If your hobbies and interests add to the evidence that you would succeed in the post on offer, give details of them, but be brief. If your hobbies are watching telly and DIY, don't waste valuable CV space on them.

Possible pitfalls

Beware of the following pitfalls:

◆ Telling the recruiter about very risky or time-consuming hobbies. An employer wants you fit, well and in work and a passion for solo round-the-world sailing trips would interfere with this.

◆ Admitting to anything that could cause a conflict of interest between you and the employer; for example, running your own part-time business.

◆ Arousing the prejudices of the reader, particularly in the areas of religion and politics. Don't make statements about your beliefs, unless these are actually relevant to the job on offer. You are unlikely to run into problems if you say, for example that you are 'an active member of my local church', but a prospective employer might well be intimidated by an announcement that you are an 'enthusiastic evangelical Christian'.

◆ Your hobbies may lead an employer, however unfairly, to stereotype you. You might be best keeping quiet about the fact that you are a train spotter or heavy metal fan.

Voluntary work

Details of voluntary work (including involvement with the Territorial Army, Police Specials, etc.) should be included in this section. The only exception to this would be where you bridged a gap between jobs with voluntary work, in which case you would show this in the Career and Achievements section of your CV.

PERSONAL DETAILS

You can decide what other personal details to give. CVs often include the following:

- nationality
- health
- driving licence details
- willingness to relocate
- date of birth
- place of birth
- marital status
- ages and numbers of children
- current salary.

Possible pitfalls

Some of your personal details may, unfortunately, lead an employer to stereotype you. You may be all too aware of the following prejudices:

- Foreign nationals will have problems with the language and work permits.

- Anyone who doesn't have a traditional English name is a foreign national.

- You need to be in perfect health to do the job.

- Only people within a narrow age band will be suitable for the post.

- The most reliable employees are married men with children.

- Parents with children at critical stages in their education won't relocate.

And so on.

Recruiters won't admit to their prejudices and may genuinely believe that they are free from them, but subconsciously the bias may still be there. If you think that a particular item may lead to unfair prejudice against you, leave it out. If you have the misfortune to meet a recruiter who stereotypes people on the basis of (for example) their age, they are much less likely to dismiss your application out of hand once they have interviewed you and found out about what you have to offer.

Nationality

If you are a foreign national but have a work permit or do not need a permit to work in this country, make a brief note of this fact. If you have been living in this country for a number of years it can be helpful to state this, as it indicates a familiarity with the culture and language.

Health

You can say that you are in excellent health as long as your ability to do your job is not impeded by any physical problems. If you cannot honestly say this, then omit this section. If you have a disability, you may choose to let the employer know that, for example, you use a wheelchair – but you are under no obligation to do so.

Driving licence

If you have a clean, full driving licence, say so. If you have penalty points on your licence, just say that you have a 'full driving licence'. Do not add the details of any penalty points unless you have specifically been asked to do so.

Relocation

If you are willing to relocate, add a short statement to this effect. Indicate which areas of the world you would be prepared to work in; for example, 'Prepared to relocate within the UK'. If you are *not* prepared to relocate, omit this section.

Date of birth

Employers like to know your date of birth. Recruiters feel that they can get a better picture of you if they know how old you are. If you have achieved a great deal at an early age, for instance, it is more likely that you are heading straight for the top. However, people make all kinds of unwarranted assumptions on the basis of your age. For example:

- This post demands a mature outlook, so the candidate must be over thirty-five.

- We need someone dynamic and energetic, so we need to recruit someone young.

- Anyone over fifty is quietly winding down to retirement.

If you don't include your date of birth, the recruiter will wonder why and may conclude that it must be because you are 'too old' for the job. It is probably best to include this information unless you are very concerned about age prejudice. Don't directly state your age, as your CV will go out of date more quickly. There is also no reason to say where you were born, as this adds no useful information for the employer.

What not to include

The following information should be added with caution, if at all:

Marital status

This should only be added if you want to capitalise on the common preconceptions that single people are more mobile and married men more dependable. Never say that you are divorced or separated, as these words may arouse unfavourable and unjustified prejudices. If your marriage has broken up, you can say that you are single.

Details of children

Many CVs include the ages, sexes and even the names of the applicant's children. Leave these out. They are irrelevant to your ability to do a job, and a prime source of prejudice, particularly if you are female. If you want to emphasise your freedom to relocate or take a job abroad, you can make a direct statement about your mobility.

Salary details

Don't give these unless you have specifically been asked to. The employer may otherwise decide that your current salary is too high for you to be seriously interested in their job, or too low for you to be senior enough to do it. If you are asked to give details of your salary, include not only your base salary but also brief details of the major benefits that you currently receive (company car, bonus, etc.), as the base salary figure on its own can be very misleading.

As this section has little bearing on your ability to do the job, leave your Personal Details until the end of your CV.

Question and answer session

'As a manager, I take a lot of time and trouble to make sure that I select people solely on their ability to do the job. Why should we be so cautious about what we put in our CVs?'

Most companies make a real effort to treat their candidates fairly, but some do not. Often recruiters are not deliberately discriminating against candidates. They just have an overly narrow picture of what the ideal candidate will be like and the discrimination is unconscious.

REFERENCES

Don't use up valuable space on your CV with details of your referees, as the employer doesn't need this information until the final stages of the selection process. Simply state 'references available on request'. The exceptions to this rule are where:

♦ your references are from deeply impressive individuals

♦ the employer has asked for details of your references in the advertisement

♦ you are looking for immediate employment or contract work and want to save the recruiter time by giving the names, addresses and telephone numbers of your referees.

Testimonial letters should not be included with senior CVs.

OTHER SECTIONS

You may want to include other sections in your CV.

Languages

If you speak more than one foreign language, create a separate section to give the details. Say whether you are fluent or whether you have a working knowledge (i.e. are reasonably competent, but not fluent). Do not include details of a language unless you have at least a working knowledge of it. Give brief details of any experience that you have had as a translator.

IT skills

Only include details if the technology is still in current use and you have a good working knowledge of it. If you are an IT specialist, you will need to create separate sections to detail the environments, programming languages, operating systems, software and hardware that you are familiar with, as part of your Career and Achievements section.

Publications

If you have published any papers, articles or books on subjects related to your profession, put the titles, dates and publisher in a separate section after your educational qualifications. If you have had a large number of works published, list only the most relevant.

Awards

List any awards that you have gained which relate to your profession or studies. If it is not immediately obvious what these are for, include a brief explanation. For example:

Institute of Pipeline Engineers, Gold Medal, XXXX
– Awarded for best research paper published each year in the field of pipeline engineering research.

Justin Meneaugh Prize, Felixtowe University, XXXX
– Awarded to the most promising final-year engineering student in a faculty of 300 students.

CASE STUDIES

Steve decides what to include in his CV

As an IT contractor, Steve includes in his CV full details of all the systems and packages that he is familiar with. Steve also has good academic qualifications, and he lets the recruiter know that he has a relevant degree, 3 A levels and 7 O levels. However, because he knows that these will be of less interest to an employer than the skills he has learned since he left university, he keeps the section on his education short.

One of Steve's strengths is the fact that he has good interpersonal skills as well as technical ability. He is sociable and likes working with people, and this is reflected in his outside interests. Steve enjoys playing sport and has been asked to join his current client's company cricket team. He includes this information in a section on his interests. Finally, Steve notes that he has a full, clean driving licence, is in excellent health and will make references available on request.

Brian decides what to include in his CV

Brian's CV focuses very much on his experience and achievements at work. He has taken the somewhat unusual step of leaving out all details of his education, because:

◆ this was over thirty years ago
◆ he gained no qualifications.

Brian therefore feels that the space would be better used by describing what he has to offer a company. He has also decided not to draw attention to his age by including his date of birth. The recruiter will be able to make a guess at how old he is by looking at the date he started work, but Brian can dispel at least one negative preconception that an employer might have about his age. As his Interests section shows, Brian is very fit and healthy, and he enjoys running and cycling.

CHECKLIST

◆ Have you included full and accurate contact details?

◆ Is your personal summary (if included) concise and meaningful?

◆ Have you included all your important professional qualifications?

◆ Have you left out irrelevant detail about your qualifications?

◆ Have you included details of your membership(s) of professional organisations?

◆ Are the details that you have given of your outside interests appropriate to your application?

◆ Are the personal details that you have given relevant?

◆ Have you included sections on all the other points that the recruiter will need to know?

POINTS TO CONSIDER

1. How important will your education and qualifications be in deciding whether you will get the job? Does the space that you have devoted to this section reflect this?

2. Will giving details of the short courses you have attended in the last few years help you to get a job?

3. What do your hobbies and interests say about you as a person?

4. Have you included anything in your CV which could lead to prejudice against you?

6

Finishing Touches

MAINTAINING YOUR PROFESSIONAL IMAGE

Your whole CV should have a highly professional image. When you go for an interview, you know that the most important thing is having the right skills and experience. But you also know how important appearances are, and that interviewers tend to make up their minds about candidates within the first few minutes of seeing them. So you take trouble over your appearance, picking a smart suit to wear, getting your hair cut, and generally making sure that you project the right image.

It's the same with your CV. Even if you have the right skills and experience, you need to make sure that these are presented in the right way. A recruiter will typically spend only a couple of minutes scanning each CV. If they cannot see the information that they need right away, your CV will go into the reject pile. If your CV is full of spelling mistakes and poorly laid out, they may conclude that you are:

- sloppy and disorganised
- not really interested in the job on offer.

Once again, your CV may be rejected. Your CV should:

- be clear and easy to read
- draw attention to your key selling points
- be attractive and professionally presented.

It should maintain your professional credibility.

CREATING AN EYE-CATCHING CV

Keeping it uncluttered

As was mentioned earlier in the book, your CV should be no longer than three pages as an absolute maximum. Don't try to get around this space constraint by cramming a mass of information on to each page in tiny print. This will make your application harder to read and prevent really important information from standing out.

If your CV looks cluttered or confusing, cut down on the amount of information that you include. Go back to your key selling points. Work out what the recruiter really needs to know about you and what can be left out. Then work out how the important information can be presented most clearly and attractively.

Choosing an attractive layout

Your CV should be visually attractive, with the text presented in neat blocks and plenty of blank space on each page. Leaving plenty of blank space improves the appearance of your CV and makes it easier to read.

Choose a consistent style in which to present your information throughout the CV. For example, you might centralise all the headings and show all dates on the left-hand side of the page. A consistent style makes it easier for the reader to find the information that they need in your CV.

Word processing packages often include templates for CVs. These often force you to put information in a set order and so it is usually better to create your own layout.

Two suggested layouts are shown in Figures 8 and 9.

Choose one businesslike style of font and stick to it – and make sure the font size is big enough so that all the information will be clearly legible even if it is photocopied and sent through the fax by the recruiter. Avoid artistic font styles and don't undermine the professional style of your CV by using graphics.

The headings for each section should be in bold or underlined to make them stand out. Keep emboldening, underlining and the use of italics elsewhere to a minimum so as not to spoil the effect. Leave wide margins and clear gaps between each block of text to make the information that you present stand out better.

Minding your language

Errors in spelling, punctuation and grammar seriously undermine the professional image that you are striving to create. Use the spellchecker on your PC (and the grammar checker, if you have one) and then get a human being to check for the errors that your computer will miss. If your application is not in your mother tongue, get it checked by a native speaker, even if you have to pay a professional translator to do this for you (you will find them listed in the *Yellow Pages*). If the recruiter finds errors they may conclude that your language skills are insufficient for the job.

NAME
Address
Home Telephone: 00000–111–2222
Mobile Telephone: 11111–222–3333

PROFILE

xxxxxxxxxxxxxxxxxxxxxxxxxxxxxxxxxxxxxxxxxxxxxxxxxxx
xxxxxxxxxxxxxxxxxxxxxxxxxxxxxxxxxxxxxxxxxxxxxxxxxxx
xxxxxxxxxxxxxxxxxxxxxxxxxxxxxxxxxxxxxxxxxxxxxxxxxx

CAREER AND ACHIEVEMENTS

Job Title   **Company Name / Address**   **Dates**
- Xxxxxxxxxxxxxxxxxxxxxxxxx
- Xxxxxxxxxxxxxxxxx
- Xxxxxxxxxxxxx

Job Title   **Company Name / Address**   **Dates**
- Xxxxxxxxxxxxxxxxxxxxxxxxx
- Xxxxxxxxxxxxxxxxx
- Xxxxxxxxxxxxx

Job Title   **Company Name / Address**   **Dates**
- Xxxxxxxxxxxxxxxxxxxxxxxxx
- Xxxxxxxxxxxxxxxxx
- Xxxxxxxxxxxxx

EDUCATION

Qualification   College   Dates
Qualification   College/School   Dates

ADDITIONAL INFORMATION

- Xxxxxxxxxxx
- Xxxxxxx
- Xxxxxxxxxxxxx
- Xxxxxxxxx

Fig. 8. Suggested CV layout 1.

NAME
Address
Home Telephone: 00000–111–2222
Mobile Telephone: 11111–222–3333

PROFILE
Xxxxxxxxxxxxxxxxxxxxxxxxxxxxxxxxxxxxxxxxxxxxxxxxxxxxx
xxxxxxxxxxxxxxxxxxxxxxxxxxxxxxxxxxxxxxxxxxxxxxxxxxxxx
xxxxxxxxxxxxxxxxxxxxxxxxxxxxxxxxxxxxxxxxxxxxxxxxxxxxx

KEY SKILLS

First skill

◆ Xxxxxxxxxxxxxxxxxxxxxxxxxxxxxxxxxxxxxxxxxxxxxxxxxx
◆ Xxxxxxxxxxxxxxxxxxxxxxxxxxxxxxxxxxxxxxxxxxxxxxxxxx
◆ Xxxxxxxxxxxxxxxxxxxxxxxxxxxxxxxxxxxxxxxxxxxxxxxxxx

Second skill

◆ Xxxxxxxxxxxxxxxxxxxxxxxxxxxxxxxxxxxxxxxxxxxxxxxxxx
◆ Xxxxxxxxxxxxxxxxxxxxxxxxxxxxxxxxxxxxxxxxxxxxxxxxxx
◆ Xxxxxxxxxxxxxxxxxxxxxxxxxxxxxxxxxxxxxxxxxxxxxxxxxx

Third skill

◆ Xxxxxxxxxxxxxxxxxxxxxxxxxxxxxxxxxxxxxxxxxxxxxxxxxx
◆ Xxxxxxxxxxxxxxxxxxxxxxxxxxxxxxxxxxxxxxxxxxxxxxxxxx
◆ Xxxxxxxxxxxxxxxxxxxxxxxxxxxxxxxxxxxxxxxxxxxxxxxxxx

CAREER SUMMARY

Job Title	Company Name / Address	Dates
Job Title	Company Name / Address	Dates
Job Title	Company Name / Address	Dates

EDUCATION

Qualification	College	Dates
Qualification	College/School	Dates

ADDITIONAL INFORMATION

◆ Xxxxxxxxxxxxx
◆ Xxxxxxxx
◆ Xxxxxxxxxxx
◆ Xxxxxxxxxxxxxxx

Fig. 9. Suggested CV layout 2.

Check to make sure that you have not used any abbreviations that will not be generally understood. If you are applying to a company or industry which is different from the one that you currently work in, make sure that you have not used any jargon that will be unfamiliar to anyone outside your firm or sector. This is especially important for people leaving the armed forces.

Going for a professional finish

Everything about your CV should show care and professionalism. You may be applying for dozens of jobs, but you don't want the recruiter to know this. Your CV should look as if it has been created especially for that one post. If you are producing paper CVs, use a laser printer and high-quality, heavy A4 paper in white or cream. Don't use coloured paper if you are applying for a senior business or professional post, and avoid photocopying your CV.

Most application forms can now be completed online. If you have to fill in an application form on paper, use a good quality pen and be prepared to make a rough draft before you complete the final version.

Send out paper CVs out in good-quality envelopes. Don't fold them and don't use your company's mail franking system.

If you are emailing your CV, avoid sending out scanned copies as these can be unreadable once they have been electronically processed by the recruiter and don't email out CVs from your work email account.

Question and answer session

'Should I email my CV or send a paper copy?'

Most job hunters will email their CVs, especially if they are applying to large organisations. An electronic CV is more easily stored and distributed and much less likely to be lost by the recruiter. However, there are circumstances where you will want to send a paper CV. A paper document has more impact than an email, which can be helpful if you are sending a speculative CV, although you will probably want to send an electronic version as well. You may also know that you are sending your CV to a technophobe who avoids using email!

'I work as a designer. I can understand that businesspeople should use the very conventional CV format that you have described above, but shouldn't I take a more creative approach? I want my CV to stand out in a very competitive job market.'

If you work in a creative industry, you do have a little more leeway to be creative in your CV, and image will be especially important. However, don't let your CV become gimmicky. A CV is a serious business document and should be presented as such – it should be presented as professionally as you would present your design ideas to a client. The best way in which you can make yourself stand out is by selling the outstanding skills that you have to offer.

USING PHOTOGRAPHS

Don't send a photograph of yourself unless you are specifically asked to. People form opinions about you very quickly from your appearance. If you do not fit the recruiter's preconceived image of what the jobholder should look like, your CV will be heading straight for the reject pile.

If you are asked to submit a photograph

Occasionally, you will be asked to send in a photograph of yourself. This is usually to help the employer remember which candidate is which at the interview stage. But be aware of the deep importance of first impressions. Senior people should never send in a snapshot or a picture taken in a photo booth. For the right result, you will need to use a professional photographer. Choose someone who is used to taking photographs for businesses. Take great care to dress in a way that will create the right impression, and let the photographer know what image you are aiming to project. Once you have a result that you are happy with, have a stock of pictures printed for future use, as reprints are expensive and take time.

Question and answer session

'I know that I'm physically attractive and photogenic. Wouldn't it help if I included a photograph?'

It might, but not necessarily. You might still not fit the image that the recruiter has of the ideal candidate, which might be based on what the last post-holder looked like.

KEEPING A COPY

Make sure that you keep a copy of each CV and covering letter that you send out. This will be crucial in helping you to prepare for interviews.

CASE STUDY

Sue revamps her CV

Sue has prepared a CV full of good selling points. However, she knows that the appearance of the document leaves something to be desired. Because she has limited time to play with, she goes to a professional office bureau which provides a CV writing service. For a modest fee, they provide Sue with an electronic CV laid out in a clear and attractive format. Sue knows that these CVs will project a thoroughly professional image and is pleased with the result.

CHECKLIST

◆ Is your CV short?

◆ Is it attractively presented and easy to read?

◆ Have you checked your spelling and grammar?

◆ Have you kept a copy for yourself?

POINTS TO CONSIDER

1. How could a different layout make your CV easier for the recruiter to read?

2. What image will the presentation of your CV give to the recruiter? Is this image appropriate?

(7)

The Covering Letter

WHAT YOUR LETTER NEEDS TO ACHIEVE

CVs and application forms should always be sent off with a covering letter or email. This is partly as a courtesy to the reader. It lets them know why you are writing in, and which vacancy you are applying for. However, your covering letter should be much more than a kind of compliments slip. The covering letter should:

◆ introduce you to the recruiter
◆ give them brief details of what you have to offer
◆ persuade the recruiter to read your CV
◆ give a great first impression.

Your covering letter or email will be the first thing from you that the employer sees, and will often be the deciding factor in whether or not the recruiter reads your CV. It is worth investing time in getting your covering letter right.

Question and answer session

'Some recruiters must get hundreds of CVs every day. Do they really read the covering letters?'

Not all recruiters read covering letters particularly now that most CVs are emailed. However, many recruiters do, and they may decide whether or not to look at the CV itself on the basis of your letter. This is particularly true for speculative CVs. Always take the time to create a professional covering letter.

'Do I still need to use covering letters now that I send all my CVs by email?'

Your CV should be sent out as an electronic attachment to an email which contains the same information that your covering letter used to. Because email is a relatively informal medium it may be appropriate for your covering email to be shorter and less formal than your covering letter used to be. It is usually best not to attach the covering letter as a separate document, as it is much less likely to be read.

What your covering letter should contain

Like your CV, the covering letter should be short and to the point. If it is sent on paper, it should easily be contained on one side of A4 and if it is emailed it should be even shorter. It will usually consist of three paragraphs containing the following information:

◆ why you are writing to the recruiter
◆ how the employer would benefit from taking you on
◆ a closing paragraph stating your wish to meet with the recruiter and an indication of when you could attend an interview.

Where your covering letter is an email to which your CV is attached, this information can be compressed into less than three paragraphs.

PARAGRAPH 1: INTRODUCING YOURSELF TO THE EMPLOYER

The first paragraph of the covering letter:

◆ greets the reader
◆ tells them why you are writing in.

Getting the introductions right

Applications should ideally be sent to a named individual, especially if you are sending in a speculative CV. A manager is more likely to read something that is addressed to them personally, and they are much more likely to read it if you have spoken to them about it first (see Chapter 1).

However, many companies with automated electronic systems for processing CVs no longer publish the name of an individual that applications should be sent to. Where an organisation does not name an individual in their advertisement or recruitment information, it is perfectly acceptable to email your CV into the central address provided with no reference to an individual.

Grabbing the reader's attention

The first paragraph needs to let the reader know why you are writing to them. If you are sending in a CV in response to an advertisement, you need to:

- identify exactly which vacancy you are interested in (there may be several)

- give the title and date of the publication in which the advertisement appeared

- quote any reference number given in the advertisement.

If you are making a speculative application, the first paragraph should say what kind of work you are looking for.

This, however, is just the bare minimum of information that any job hunter should give as a courtesy. Senior people need to go further. You need to use this opportunity to get the reader's attention and sell yourself to them. In this paragraph you should:

- remind them of any contact you have had in the past (this makes it much more likely they will read on)

- express your great interest in working for them.

If you have spoken to the recruiter about the possibility of working with them, refer back to the conversation and thank them for taking the time to speak to you.

Examples

Dear Charles,

It was good to meet you last week at the Software Engineering conference. I was very interested by what you had to say about the possibility of contract work with Megaco . . .

Dear Miss Smith,

Thank you for taking the time to talk to me yesterday about your vacancy for a Store Manager in your Reading outlet. . .

Showing a real interest

The next step is to demonstrate both that you have a knowledge of what the company needs and your interest in working for them. For example:

- *I have watched your recent rapid expansion in the insurance market with great interest . . .*

- *As an experienced software engineer, I was very interested to hear that your company is diversifying into the production of software packages for the small business market . . .*

Your interest must sound genuine, so don't go over the top. If you tell the employer that your life's ambition has been to gain a job in the accounts department of Consolidated Widgets, they are unlikely to believe you. Don't use identical phrases on all the letters that you send out. You will need to find out the real issues facing the company if you are to establish any credibility.

Question and answer session

'I am very busy in my current job and simply don't have time to do research into each company that I apply to. What should I say in this section?'

If you don't have the time to do some real research, then don't try to guess the challenges of the company. Remember that you will be talking to the experts in that particular field! You could simply say 'I was very interested by your advertisement for a Marketing Manager in "The Daily Echo" . . .' However, the more you can show that you know about the company, the greater your chances of being called for interview. And the more senior you are, the more you will be expected to know if you are going to stand a chance of being selected.

Remembering the employer's interests

Remember that employers will be interested in how you could help them – not in how they could further your career. The reason you are telling the recruiter how interested you are is because employers benefit from taking on people who are enthusiastic about the job on offer. Avoid using the following approaches:

◆ *I feel that I would be able to gain valuable experience with your company . . .*

◆ *Having gained several years of experience in business law, I am now keen to develop my career further in a large partnership such as yours . . .*

◆ *This is an area in which I have always wanted to develop my skills. . .*

PARAGRAPH 2: SAYING WHAT YOU HAVE TO OFFER

In the second paragraph, tell the employer how they would benefit from taking you on. It is this paragraph that is going to be of most interest to the recruiter and will make them decide whether or not they are going to read your CV. Draw the recruiter's attention to two or three of your key selling points that will be of most interest to them. Keep this brief – if you try to rewrite everything on your CV, the important points will be lost in a mass of detail.

Presenting your skills and experience

Avoid empty hype. Give concrete information on the skills and experience that you have and perhaps some information on one of your major achievements – something to get the reader's attention and make them look at your CV to find out more about you. For example:

◆ *During my three years as production manager with Able Engineering, I reduced product defects by 30% . . .*

◆ *As you can see from my CV, I have worked in retailing for five years . . .*

◆ *I am a seasoned petroleum engineer, with experience of working in North Africa and the Middle East . . .*

Choose points that will be of particular interest to the company, perhaps because you have specific skills which that company needs, or because in your work for another organisation you have solved a problem that the recruiter now faces. The more senior the post, the more you will need to show that you understand the opportunities and challenges facing the new organisation.

Being tactful

While you want to show awareness of the challenges that the recruiting company is facing, avoid saying straight out that you understand that they have a problem. Managers will know only too well the problems that they face and will not enjoy being told outright that (for example) their organisation is overstaffed and customer complaints are going through the roof. This is especially true if these areas are their responsibility. Keep your statements neutral. For example:

◆ *While at Zedco Limited, I reduced staff costs by 25% ...*

◆ *I have extensive experience in improving customer service in a competitive marketplace ...*

Avoid lecturing the employer on how to run their business. All too many covering letters include statements such as 'reducing overheads is important to the efficient running of a business ...' or 'improving customer service will be vital if your business is to succeed ...'. You can assume that the employer already knows this!

Making sure your CV backs your letter up

Your covering letter will be telling the employer about your extensive experience, skills and achievements. To maintain your credibility, make sure that all the claims you make are backed up with evidence in your CV.

PARAGRAPH 3: SETTING THE SCENE FOR THE NEXT STAGE

Don't let your letter or email tail off with a lame 'yours sincerely'. Close with a strong positive phrase setting the scene for the next stage – the recruiter asking you to attend an interview. For example:

◆ *I would welcome the opportunity to discuss this with you further. I will be on leave in the UK between 1st and 14th June and could attend an interview at any time during this fortnight.*

◆ *I look forward to meeting you and could attend an interview at short notice.*

Question and answer session

'I read an American book which suggested that you should tell the employer that you look forward to meeting them and will be contacting them shortly to make the arrangements. This guarantees you an interview and shows them how dynamic and proactive you are. Do you think this is a good idea?'

What looks proactive in the USA is unacceptably pushy here. Unless you're looking for a post in cold-call sales, the recruiter is likely to decide that you just aren't their type. Always leave it up to the recruiter to decide if they would like to see you. You could, however, follow up the speculative CV with a call to check that the employer has received your CV and to ask politely if they would like to see you.

Finishing off

Where you are sending a paper covering letter, the ending should be 'Yours sincerely' if you are writing to a named individual. If you have written to 'Dear Sir/Madam', then the ending is 'Yours faithfully'. Beneath this should come your signature (preferably in ink, which conveys a more professional image than biro) and then your name typed or printed in full.

Emails can be less formal. Where you have already spoken to the recruiter, it may be appropriate to end your email with 'Best Regards' and your name and contact details.

PRODUCING YOUR COVERING LETTER

If you are sending your covering letters out on paper, they should be produced using a word processor and high quality printer, using the same paper and font as the CV. Like your CV, your covering letter should be well laid-out, clear and easy to read. The paper should be white or cream. Never used lined paper or stationery from your existing employer.

CASE STUDY

Sue's first attempt at a covering email is shown in Figure 10.

There is a number of areas where it could be improved:

◆ A letter addressed to 'Dear Sir/Madam' is much less likely to be read than one addressed to a named individual, and the email subject is very vague.

◆ A covering letter should not say that you feel that you haven't got all the skills and experience needed for the role. It should deal with your strengths.

Subject: recruitment

Dear Sir or Madam,

Please find my CV attached for your consideration.

I have spent the last eleven years working as a maintenance manager. I am now keen to expand my skills and knowledge by working as a facilities manager. While I have not worked as a facilities manager before, I feel that my background and skills mean that I am ideally suited to the role. A large company such as yours would offer me excellent development opportunities.

If you have any suitable vacancies please do not hesitate to contact me.

Yours faithfully,

Susan Brown

Fig. 10. Sue's first attempt at a covering email.

- Sue has given one of her selling points – that she has eleven years' experience of maintenance management. But by stating that she is a maintenance manager she is reinforcing the point that she hasn't got experience as a *facilities* manager.

- As Sue has just said that she has not worked as a facilities manager, saying that she feels she is ideally suited to the role sounds a bit presumptuous.

- Sue says that she has the right skills and background for the job but she doesn't give any details. As this is a speculative CV, the employer may well not read further and find out what she has to offer.

◆ A covering letter or email should concentrate not on what the company can offer you but on what you can offer them. This is what a recruiter is interested in!

Sue's final covering email (see Figure 11) has a very much higher chance of success:

Application for facilities management post

Dear Alan Green,

Thank you for taking the time to talk to me this morning. I was very interested to hear that Pizza Place will be opening their new head office in Shorely early next year and that you will be recruiting a facilities manager for the site. I successfully prepared the Dataco head office for occupation within budget and to a tight deadline. I also have managed all aspects of maintenance for 6 Dataco offices, accommodating 800 staff. Setting up and running the facilities management department at your new head office would be a challenge that I would relish.

I have attached my CV, which I hope you will find of interest. The opportunity to discuss this post further with you would be very welcome.

Yours sincerely,

Susan Brown (Mrs)

home phone 00000 111 2222
mobile 11111 222 3333
email sb7006@ameritech.com

24 Mounds Road
Walton
Hampshire PT29 3QE

Fig. 11. Sue's final covering email.

◆ Sue has found out which company is going to occupy a new office complex being built in her area, identified the property manager within that company *and* spoken to him to ascertain that he will need a facilities manager. Her CV is going to the right person and there is a very good chance that it will be read. The subject of the email is stated clearly which will make it easy for it to be identified.

◆ Sue has set the right tone by thanking Alan Green for taking the time to speak to her. The reader is also tactfully reminded of what their discussion was about.

◆ Sue shows that she can offer the skills that Pizza Place needs in getting the new head office up and running and expresses enthusiasm for the job.

◆ The email finishes in a positive manner, and points the way for Alan Green to invite her for interview.

CHECKLIST

◆ Have you identified who or where to send your CV to?

◆ Does your letter/email express enthusiasm at the idea of working for the employer?

◆ Does your letter/email show a genuine understanding of the needs of the business?

◆ Have you shown the employer what you can offer them?

◆ Does your letter/email have a strong positive ending?

POINTS TO CONSIDER

1. If you were a recruiter, what would you want to see on a covering letter or email?

2. What would get your attention and make you read further?

3. What would make you delete the email or throw away the letter with the CV unread?

8

The Next Step

As soon as you have sent your CV off, you need to start preparing for the next stage – the call for interviews. You may be asked to attend interviews at short notice (particularly if you are looking for contract work) so it pays to be ready.

ARRANGING YOUR ANSWERING SERVICE

You want to give a professional impression if the recruiter calls you at home or on your mobile. Make sure that your answerphone message is appropriately businesslike. If you have children who may answer the phone, make sure that they understand the importance of taking down messages accurately and then passing them on.

Check your answerphone and 'calls missed' messages at least once a day. There is nothing more frustrating for a recruiter than being unable to track someone down. Similarly, if you have given out your email address, make sure that you check your inbox daily.

GETTING YOUR PAPERWORK IN ORDER

Make sure that you have all the documents that you will need to show the recruiter if you are offered the job. You will not convey the right impression if you realise at the last minute that you have lost a vital certificate and have to wait for the issuing body to send a new copy through. Information that you are likely to have to show the employer includes:

- copies of your qualification certificates

- proof that you have the right to live and work in this country (note: current UK Home Office guidelines mean that many companies ask **all** new recruits to prove they have the right to work in Britain – not just foreign nationals)

- if you are looking for work abroad or applying for a post in an industry where security is crucial, your birth certificate and an up-to-date passport

- proof that you have completed any safety training mandatory in your industry

- for those working in the creative professions, samples of previous work (make sure that you don't show the recruiter something which should be kept confidential).

Take two copies of your CV to the interview. One is for yourself, and the other for the interviewer just in case their copy has gone astray.

ARRANGING YOUR REFERENCES

Decide at this point who you will ask to give you a reference, and whether this might give rise to any problems that you could resolve now.

Choosing your referees

You will need references from at least two people. References for senior posts should always be from people who have known you at work and should include your last manager. Wherever possible, check beforehand that the person you have named is happy to provide you with a reference – although for obvious reasons it will not be possible to do this where the referee is your current manager. Recruiters will only contact your referees when they have made or are on the point of making you a firm job offer, and will let you know before they do so. This gives you a chance to give some advance warning to your referee. Give your referees a copy of your CV to assist them when the time comes for them to provide the reference.

Possible problems

If you are asked to provide names of referees and do not give the name of a manager from your last job, you will arouse the suspicions of the recruiter. If you did not leave your last employer on good terms, it is still worth speaking to them to see if they would be prepared to give you an acceptable reference. Firms are often unwilling to give a bad reference and most will be prepared at least to give a new employer a carefully noncommittal account of you. If you are in the process of negotiating your departure from the firm, provision of a reference is an essential point in the discussions.

If your employer refuses to give you an acceptable reference, you will need to explain to the recruiter that you had a problem with your last employer and would therefore like to offer alternative references. In this situation you should make every effort to ensure that your alternative references are really good ones.

PREPARING YOURSELF PERSONALLY

Job hunting is a stressful business, especially if you do not have the security of an ongoing permanent job to fall back on. You will inevitably encounter rejections along the way, and this will stir up insecurities. Rationally, you know that you have the skills and experience that you need. Even so, after a few rejections you may start to worry about whether you are good enough.

Be prepared for this. Eliminate as many other sources of stress from your life as possible, and plan time out to relax. Find sources of support to help you in your search for work. These could be:

- family
- friends
- other job seekers.

An informal support group of other job seekers can be very helpful in maintaining your morale.

Plan a schedule of what actions you are going to take and when in your search for work. For example, you may decide to set target dates for completing your CV, calling up a certain number of your contacts, and registering with agencies. If you are currently working, you will need to set aside specific times in which to conduct your jobsearch. It is also crucial to plan and set yourself targets if you are not working. Otherwise you may quickly be diverted onto other tasks: looking for a new senior role is a full-time job.

PREPARING FOR YOUR INTERVIEW

Putting together a CV is a great first step in this preparation process. While you have been creating your CV you have:

- researched your target employer/industry
- identified your strongest points
- practised the art of talking positively about yourself and your achievements
- taken a realistic look at what your weaker points are.

Completing your research

At a senior level you are expected to demonstrate at your
interview a real understanding of the company and industry in
which you are applying to work. You will usually have done some
research into the organisation before you compile your CV.
However, some job advertisements do not give the name of the
recruiting company. You will only be told this if and when you
are called for interview, and will then need to do your research at
this stage. If you are applying for a position in a commercial
organisation, make sure that you can talk knowledgeably about
the company's:

◆ financial position
◆ products and services
◆ culture
◆ likely future direction
◆ strengths, weaknesses, opportunities and threats
◆ competitors.

If you are a professional applying to work in a partnership, you
will need to be able to discuss:

◆ current and expected developments in your specialist field
◆ how your skills could help the partnership move forward.

Revisiting your strong points

Take another look at your key selling points. These are the areas
that you will want your interview to concentrate on. Decide:

◆ how you are going to ensure that each point is covered in the
  discussion

- what you want to tell the interviewer about each point
- the most positive way in which to sell each of your key skills.

The interview is your chance to expand on your achievements in the detail that you had to leave out of the CV. Remember that the interviewer will often want to probe not just what you have achieved but how you achieved it. For example, if your CV shows that you doubled sales in your area within three years, the interviewer will want to know how you went about this. Did you reach these figures through developing positive and sustainable relationships with customers or through aggressive hard sell to people who will never order again? Did you manage to maintain harmonious relations with the production department throughout or did you land them with orders that they couldn't fill?

Revisit your strong points just before the interview. This will remind you of the points that you want to talk about in the interview and looking at all your past achievements will be a great confidence booster.

Taking a look at your weaker areas

It is a lot harder to hide weaknesses in an interview than it is in a CV. Think through how you will answer questions on any areas that an interviewer might see as a weakness. For each of these areas you will need to be able to show how:

- an apparent weakness could be turned to an advantage, and/or
- you have compensating strengths, and/or
- you will overcome the weakness, and/or
- you will minimise the effect that the weakness has on the organisation.

For example:

Possible problem – you have only ever worked for one company.
Response – sell the fact that you are steady and reliable, and have
built up a real depth of knowledge that can be transferred to the
recruiting firm.

Possible problem – you are applying for an overseas assignment
but have never worked abroad before.
Response – tell the interviewer about the year you spent studying
abroad as part of your degree course and how well you adapted to
life overseas. Build on this by talking about the many short
business trips abroad that you have made.

Possible problem – although you have many years of experience in
finance, you never finished your accountancy qualifications. You
know that the recruiter would prefer someone who is fully
qualified.
Response – sell your experience and the fact that you are
committed to gaining professional accreditation in the near future.

Possible problem – although you have many years of retail
experience, this has all been in stores selling clothing and
footwear. You have never managed a supermarket before.
Response – talk about your transferable skills and how interested
you are in the fresh challenge of food retailing.

You might decide to talk about your solution before the manager
raises the fact that there might be a problem or in case they do

not even raise the issue. This is a valuable tactic where you know that an employer may make unfounded assumptions about you. For example:

Possible problem – You are a 35-year-old woman applying for a job which will involve relocating to the other end of the country. You know that if you were a man, they would simply assume that your partner would move to follow your career. Because you are a woman, they may assume that there will be a problem but not ask you about the issue outright.

Response – You have two options here:

◆ You may decide that as you are a mature professional, the recruiter can take it for granted that the issue of relocation is one that you will have addressed before you even applied for the job. This is a perfectly legitimate stance to take.

◆ You may accept that the recruiter is likely (perhaps quite unconsciously) to be making discriminatory assumptions about your ability to relocate. You therefore decide to talk during the interview about the fact that both you and your husband would enjoy moving to Scotland and that his home-based job means that you could do this at short notice.

Building up your interview skills

Take a realistic look at how good your interview skills are and whether these could be improved. You could increase your chances of success through:

◆ Practising interviews with a friend who can be trusted to give useful feedback, or better still a career consultant.

◆ Reading one of the excellent books on the market on improving interview skills. If you are applying for a job in the UK, make sure that you buy a book produced for British rather than American readers.

Preparing to create the right impression

Most interviewers make up their mind about the suitability of a candidate within the first few minutes of the interview, and much of this is based on the appearance of the candidate. Make sure that your clothes, briefcase, accessories and haircut are all smart and professional and project the right image.

MAKING THE MOST OF YOUR MARKETING DOCUMENT

Once you have won the post that you want, don't throw your CV away or put it in the bottom of a drawer and forget about it. Developing your career is an ongoing process. Think about whether there is anything that you could do now that would be a real addition to your CV the next time you are looking for work.

◆ Is there a strong point that you could develop further?
◆ Is there a weakness that you should work on?
◆ Do you need to build up a better network of contacts?

Revisit your CV every six months or so (more if you work on short-term contracts) to update it. As you have just found out, putting together a winning CV is a time-consuming business. There is nothing more frustrating than finding out about a great new position and not having the time to apply for it. Keep your CV up to date. The next time that you find out about a promising new career opportunity, you'll be ready to meet it.

CASE STUDIES
Steve prepares himself

As a contractor, Steve knows the importance of being able to provide hiring companies with all the information they ask for at short notice. He keeps everything that he is likely to need together in one file. When he moves from his rented flat in London to his new house in Yorkshire, he makes sure that he keeps this file with him instead of leaving it with the rest of his belongings for the removals firm to transport. Steve contacts all the agencies that he works with in advance, to let them know the date of the move and his new address and phone number. He makes sure that his phone, fax and internet connection are working as soon as he moves in and on the day of the move he keeps his mobile switched on all day, just in case!

Sue gets ready for the interview

Sue is a confident communicator in normal working situations, but feels slightly nervous about her forthcoming interview with Pizza Place. She therefore spends some time thinking about all the awkward questions that she could be asked and rehearsing great answers. Because she does not normally dress smartly for work (her job is too hands-on to make this practical) Sue also invests in a new suit for the occasion.

CHECKLIST

◆ Do your family know that you may get calls from future employers at home?

◆ Are you checking your answerphone and emails regularly?

◆ Have you got all the paperwork you will need to show an employer?

- Have you decided who you will ask for references?

- Are you prepared to deal with the stress of job hunting?

- Have you researched the employer thoroughly?

- Have you decided how to talk about your strengths and weaknesses at interviews?

POINTS TO CONSIDER

1. What could you do to improve your interview skills?

2. How will you make sure that you project the right image at your interview?

9

Postscript – Case Studies

Steve

Steve has several offers in the pipeline before he moves to Yorkshire, and is delighted to be offered a project management contract with a major accountancy firm shortly after his arrival. Well before the six-month contract is complete, he has again revamped his CV and is again talking to employment agencies. He also decides to do a management qualification by distance learning to enhance his project management skills.

Sue

Alan Green, the property manager for Pizza Place, had not been planning to recruit from outside the company for the role of facilities manager at their new head office. While he had been too busy to look seriously into the options, he was thinking of perhaps moving one of his existing team into the role as a development opportunity. There were a couple of people based in Birmingham and Liverpool who might have been suitable. Alan is very interested to get a call from a good candidate living locally – here's a chance to save on his relocation budget! Following an interview, he offers Sue the job.

Brian

Brian is relieved to be offered the temporary contract at Zipco, as he only has a few weeks left in his old job. However, it is a shock to the system to leave British Engineering after so many years. Everything is done differently in his new role, he feels insecure as a contractor, and he hates the weekly commute to Scotland from the south of England. But after a few months, he finds to his surprise that he is starting to enjoy the change from his comfortable old routine.

Brian has started studying for a professional qualification by distance learning to increase his marketability. He starts his search for a new post well before the end of the Zipco contract. Brian has kept in touch with the supplier of the human resources software that they used at British Engineering and is delighted to get a call from his contact there. They have had a surge of new orders and need a mobile contractor to train buyers in how the system works – would Brian be interested? He takes on the role, and six months later he is in Beijing teaching the system to Chinese government officials through a translator. Brian decides that he finds life as a contractor much more interesting and enjoyable than he ever thought he would!

The following pages show sample CVs.

Alison Smith
56, Long Street, Northtown, Staffordshire SR5 6CD
Home Telephone: 11111 – 999 – 8888
Mobile: 88888 – 999 – 0000
Email: as2067@ameritech.com

PROFILE

A Production Manager with twenty years' experience in the ceramics industry and an excellent track record of introducing improvements. Chartered Engineer and MBA graduate.

CAREER AND ACHIEVEMENTS

Production Manager **Bowes China Ltd** **Dec XX – April XX**
Northtown, Staffs

◆ Reporting to the Director and General Manager, managing the production of 400 domestic china products on 5 production lines during a time of expansion for the company.

◆ Leading a production team of 100, working a 2-shift system. Over three years, reducing absenteeism by 25% and staff turnover by 20% by setting targets, improving recruitment and training methods, improving communication with the workforce and effectively handling individual problem cases.

◆ Saving the company £100,000 per annum through reducing the number of products failed at quality inspection, by introducing quality circles and making technical changes and management changes identified by these circles.

◆ Introducing Quality Standard ISO 9001 to the Production Department and ensuring full compliance with this standard, which has helped Bowes China win new orders with clients.

◆ Managing the installation of new equipment worth £3 million to a tight schedule to ensure that new orders could be met.

Production Supervisor **Bowes China Ltd** **March XX – Dec XX**
Northtown, Staffs

◆ Reporting to the Production Manager, managing 2 production lines and a team of 40 staff.

◆ Designing and introducing a production information reporting system used throughout the department to monitor production quantities, quality standards and safety statistics.

◆ Reducing lost time accidents in the team by 30% through active leadership and communication on safety issues.

Research Technician   **Bowes China Ltd**   **Sept XX – Feb XX**
                                    Northtown, Staffs

- Undertaking technical investigations into the causes of production faults and proposing solutions to the Production Manager.
- Assisting line managers to make modifications to equipment and working methods to improve production.
- Researching technical developments within the industry and reporting to management on those of probable benefit to the company.
- Undertaking factory trials of new lines and modified technology to ensure changes introduced smoothly.

EDUCATION

MBA	Midlands University	XXXX – XXXX (part-time study)
BSc (Hons) 2:2 Mechanical Engineering	West Wales University	XXXX – XXXX
3 A levels	Broadwick School, Crewe	XXXX – XXXX

FURTHER TRAINING

- Diploma in Quality Management awarded by Midlands College XXXX
- Certificate in Supervisory Skills awarded by Midlands College XXXX
- Training on computer programming and the Multisoft products suite

ADDITIONAL INFORMATION

- Date of birth XX/XX/XX
- Full, clean driving licence
- Excellent health
- References available on request

SHARON JONES
12 Ellesmere Gardens, Heaton, Lancashire MW12 345
Mobile: 0000 – 1111 – 2222
Email: s_green500@maillink.com

PROFILE

A dedicated and experienced Assistant Head of English, who enjoys building a team to provide the best possible teaching to all pupils and is ready to make the step to the role of Head of Department.

CAREER AND ACHIEVEMENTS

Assistant Head of English	**Park Road Comprehensive School, Heaton, Lancashire**	**Sept XX – Present**

Park Road Comprehensive School is a mixed-sex, urban school rated as 'excellent' by Ofsted. There are 900 pupils, with 150 in the sixth form.

- With the Head of English, managing a team of 4 teachers to provide stimulating and appropriate teaching of English Language and Literature to pupils with a wide range of abilities. The team's achievements include:
  - Raising the school's English Language and Literature GCSE grade A–C pass rates from 40% to 60% within 4 years through managing the introduction of regular testing and mock examinations, providing special needs support where needed, choosing a syllabus which pupils find interesting and relevant and providing training in study skills.
  - Raising the number of pupils choosing to take 'A' level English by 25% within 4 years.
- Delivering the National Curriculum to pupils at Key Stages 3 and 4. Preparing students for GCSE and 'A' level examinations.
- Running the school drama club, which regularly produces popular plays including 'The Crucible' and 'A Midsummer Night's Dream'.
- Setting up and running study skills courses for students at GCSE and 'A' level.

Teacher of English	**Park Road Comprehensive School**	**Sept XX – July XX**

- Teaching English Language and Literature to pupils at all levels of ability.
- Organising school trips of up to 50 pupils to see plays in local theatres.
- Working as one of a team of 3 teachers running the drama club.

| **Exchange Teacher** | **Woolalong School, Australia** | **Sept XX – July XX** |

◆ Expanding my horizons as one of a few teachers selected to take part in an exchange programme with Australian schools.

| **Teacher of English** | **Park Road Comprehensive School** | **Sept XX – July XX** |

◆ Please see above

| **Teaching Experience** | **Town Road Secondary School, London** | **XXXX** |

◆ Teaching English to a challenging group of pupils in an inner-city school as part of my PGCE course.

EDUCATION

Postgraduate Certificate of Education (Pass)	Liverpool College	XXXX–XXXX
English BA (Hons) Class 2:1	Midfield University	XXXX–XXXX
A level English (B), Drama (B) and French (B)	St. Swithin's School Lancaster	XXXX–XXXX

ADDITIONAL INFORMATION

◆ Date of birth XX/XX/XX
◆ Full clean driving licence; experienced minibus driver
◆ Excellent health
◆ References available on request
◆ My main hobby is music. I play the piano (grade 5) and flute (grade 4), often in support of school productions and activities. I also enjoy singing and am a very active member of a church choir.

TOM EVANS
Flat 12, 37 West Street, London, NE1 2AB
Home Telephone: 0000 – 111 – 2222
Mobile Telephone: 1111 – 222 – 3333
Email: te@mailline.com

PROFILE

A versatile and creative Graphic Designer who has made a major contribution to nationwide promotional campaigns. Skilled in the design of marketing, advertising, packaging and corporate communication materials including internet and intranet webpages. An effective team manager, able to manage projects from concept to production and to meet tight deadlines.

KEY SKILLS

Design of Marketing Materials

- Design of marketing materials from concept through to delivery of the finished product, including posters, brochures, flyers, magazine advertisements, websites and point-of-sale materials, supporting major nationwide advertising campaigns.
- Experienced in working solo and as part of an agency or client team.
- Illustration and copywriting for all types of marketing materials.
- Experienced in producing materials for both retail and business-to-business advertising.
- Clients include Fizzco drinks (Tropical Sun campaign – runner up in the Food Advertising Industry Awards) Sabre Cars (Z model launch) and Datacom Computers.

Packaging Design

- Design of product packaging for a wide variety of retail and business-to-business goods, including luxury, child-oriented, fast-moving and perishable goods.
- Clients include The Old-Fashioned Sweet Company (range of chocolate confectionery), KidKo Toys (Holly Dolls, Plastibricks), The American Coffee Co. (disposable cups, napkins) and Timeco (packaging for watches).

Corporate Branding and Communications

- Design of corporate logos, letterheads, business cards and business gifts consistent with company style and identity for businesses including British Utilities and KidKo.
- Managing corporate rebranding exercises for Sunshine Holidays and the Disabled Children's Foundation to ensure effective communication of the organisation's image to customers, employees and clients.

- Designing and producing in-house journals and other in-house communication materials for major companies including British Utilities (30,000 employees) and Sabre Cars (15,000 employees).

Internet and Intranet Design
- Managing the design of/personally designing websites, including the management of information technology specialists working on design teams.
- Delivering internet sites attracting up to 10,000 hits per day to clients including The Consumer Bureau and the Heart Research Foundation. (Sites can be viewed at www.complaints.co and www.hrf.co
- Producing Intranets to communicate corporate messages to the employees of companies targeting up to 30,000 staff, including Insureco, British Utilities and Wham Records.

Management
- Managing teams of up to 8 design staff, working on multiple projects and to tight deadlines in both agency and in-house situations.
- Managing the subcontracting of work to photographers, illustrators, copywriters and printers to ensure high standards achieved and target delivery dates met.

CAREER SUMMARY

Associate Design Director	Imageworks	Feb XX – Present
Corporate Communications Manager	British Utilities	March XX – Feb XX
Design Manager	Sabre Cars	May XX – March XX
Design Consultant	Adco	Dec XX – May XX
Senior Designer	Adco	May XX – Dec XX
Full-time Freelancer	New Look	Nov XX – May XX
Senior Designer	The Image Shop	July XX – Nov XX
Designer	Graphco	Sept XX – July XX

Between XXXX and XXXX I also undertook numerous freelance commissions.

EDUCATION

BTEC HND in Graphic Design	Fens College	XXXX – XXXX
BTEC HNC in Graphic Design	Fens College	XXXX – XXXX
A level Art, 6 O levels	Amborne School	XXXX – XXXX

ADDITIONAL INFORMATION

- Skilled in a wide variety of design packages and internet authoring software, including Photoworks, Drawsoft and Webgraph
- Date of birth XX/XX/XX
- Willing to work anywhere within Europe and North America
- Excellent references available on request

SANJAY PATEL
18, South Street, Glasgow, GL12 3BC
Email: sp300@ameritech.com
Mobile 43210 – 9876543

An experienced Management Accountant with full CIMA qualifications. Strong track record of improving processes with the best use of management information systems. Highly adaptable team player with experience in retail, engineering, local government and the health service.

Key skills and achievements

Management information systems
- Working with systems in a wide range of organisations to develop and improve financial and business processes. Strong on managing projects within budgets and deadlines.
- Sourcing, implementing and troubleshooting new accountancy software systems for Clothesco and Newtech. Producing full documentation and training manuals and training a total of 60 users.
- Designing, testing and implementing of a major networked time management system for British Engineering to capture, reconcile and analyse employee time bookings including the successful management of complex interfaces with payroll and client billing systems.
- Designing and programming a laptop insurance quotation system for mobile financial advisers at Anglo Insurance plc to allow instant insurance quotes to be given.
- Managing a team of 4 to develop for Electricorp a sales database of customer information for 2 million households for use in expanding the company's expansion into gas and water supplies, including commission management, links with the payroll system and automated sales reporting.

Financial procedures and controls
- Setting up and improving accounting procedures to ensure sound financial controls in both private and public sector organisations. Improving corporate governance, risk management and internal controls.
- Setting up all accountancy procedures and controls for e-Shop, a new online PC games retailer with projected £3 million turnover.
- Redesigning accountancy policies and procedures for Newhomes Estate Agency to comply with parent company procedures following their takeover by Megabank.
- Rewriting and implementing updated costs monitoring systems for Prestwich Council.
- Auditing financial systems for the East Glasgow Hospitals Trust and Clothesco.

Financial statements

- Managing teams or working solo to produce accurate and timely financial statements including weekly/monthly/year-end profit and loss; budgets and forecasts; cash flow statements; variance analyses and commentaries.
- Developing fixed assets registers of the assets of Newhomes estate agency as part of the Megabank takeover.
- Producing company tax and VAT returns for companies including Gasco Garages and e-Shop.

Information Systems

- Financial software: Accucount, NewCount, Megacalc
- Environments: Tech 6.1, Megatech, Opsys
- Programming languages: Babel, Intlang
- Data mining: Searchout

Career Summary

Fixed term contracts: a wide variety of companies May XX – present including:

- Clothesco
- Anglo Insurance
- Megabank
- East Glasgow Hospitals Trust
- Prestwich Council.

Senior Management Accountant	Newtech	June XX – May XX
Management Accountant	Electricorp	Sept XX – June XX
Accountant	British Engineering	April XX – August XX
Graduate Trainee	British Engineering	Sept XX – April XX

Education

CIMA qualifications (p/time)	Prestwich Polytechnic	XX – XX
BSc (Hons) Business Studies	Prestwich Polytechnic	XX – XX
8 O levels, 3 A levels	Prestwich Grammar School	XX – XX

Other information

- Preferred location – Scotland
- Fluent spoken and written Hindi
- Full driving licence
- DOB XX/XX/XX
- Excellent references available on request

JANE HARRIS
21, Short Street, Coasttown, CT15 9BL
Email: JH3456@ameritech.com
Home Phone 1234 - 098765
Mobile 56789 – 012345

An experienced **Legal Manager** and **Solicitor** looking for a new role leading an in-house legal department.

CAREER AND ACHIEVEMENTS

| **Legal Manager** | **Servicerite** | **Nov XX – Sept XX** |

Servicerite provides electrical, plumbing and maintenance services on a contract basis to commercial customers nationwide. As Legal Manager I report into the Finance Director, managing a team of 2 legally qualified staff, providing a full support service on commercial and employment law.

◆ Conducting litigation and representing the company in arbitration, mediation and adjudication including debt recovery issues and employment tribunals.

◆ Risk analysis for all major tenders and legal support on negotiations with client companies.

◆ Drafting of contracts for services bought into Servicerite. Successfully handling TUPE issues. Saved £40,000 per annum as a result of changing provision of external legal services by bringing some services in-house and setting up alliances with selected legal firms.

◆ Providing a full employment law advisory service for a workforce of 1,500 staff, including issuing new employment contracts and advising on the closure of the final pension scheme to new members.

◆ Conducting in-house training on risk management and employment law.

◆ Monitoring legal changes, advising management and amending processes and documentation.

Senior Solicitor	**Martin & Jones,**	**Nov XX – Sept XX**
Solicitor	**Newtown**	**April XX – Nov XX**
Trainee Solicitor		**Oct XX – April XX**

Martin and Jones is one of the most respected legal firms in the south-east with strengths in commercial and employment law.

I specialised in commercial law, advising a wide range of clients including blue-chip companies.

◆ Advising clients on acquisitions, mergers, takeovers, management buyouts, joint ventures and reorganisations, including acquisitions and disposals with values of up to £120 million.

◆ Acting for clients in relation to secured and unsecured lending, negotiating with banks and reviewing lending agreements.

◆ Advising on share sales and acquisitions.

- Drafting contracts and contracts for services, joint venture agreements, agency agreements, licensing and royalty agreements and security documents.
- Advising on new legislation including the Data Protection Act, and the impact of new employment legislation and the Human Rights Act.
- Providing in-house training and writing legal updates for clients on a variety of commercial law issues.

Legal training/career break   **Jan XX – Sept XX**
Career break to look after my young family followed by legal training.

Personnel Adviser   **Electricorp**   **Sept XX – Jan XX**
Providing a full personnel support service to a business unit of 500 people within Electricorp, including the provision of advice to managers on employment law and representing the company at industrial tribunals.

Early Career   **Electricorp**   **August XX – Sept XX**
I worked my way up from the position of Junior Secretary to Personnel Adviser.

QUALIFICATIONS

Legal Practice Course – Commendation	Newtown College of Law	XX – XX
Common Professional Examination	Newtown College of Law	XX – XX
LLB (Hons) Law	Newtown University	XX – XX
Secretarial diploma	Smalltown College	XX – XX
7 O levels, 3 'A' levels	Smalltown Grammar School	XX – XX

OTHER INFORMATION

- Working knowledge of French
- Full driving licence
- DOB XX/XX/XX
- Excellent references available on request

Glossary

ASSC. Association of Search and Selection Consultancies.

Blue chip. A business which is listed on the stock exchange and which has a sound reputation amongst investors.

CIPD. Chartered Institute of Personnel and Development, the professional body for HR managers.

Covering letter. The letter that goes out with a CV or application form.

CV. Curriculum vitae: Latin for 'the course of one's life'.

CV banks. An internet site where CVs are stored for interested recruiters to view.

H.R. Human Resources – the personnel department.

K. An abbreviation for a thousand pounds, often used in job advertisements. £30K (for example) is £30,000.

Locum. A professional who temporarily fills the post of another member of their profession.

OTE. On track earnings. Usually quoted for sales jobs where the amount of your pay depends on sales made.

Outplacement consultant. A career consultant retained to help those being made redundant from a company.

REC Recruitment and Employment Confederation.

Résumé Another word for CV used by North American organisations.

Speculative CV. A CV sent by a job hunter enquiring whether an organisation has a suitable vacancy, rather than one sent in reply to a job advertisement.

Further Reading

General

The Job Hunter's Handbook, *An A–Z of Tried and Tested Tips*, David Greenwood (Kogan Page).

What Colour is Your Parachute?, Richard Nelson Bolles, Mark Emery (Ten Speed Press), US.

Careers

The Career Change Handbook, Graham Green (How To Books).

Planning a Career Change, Judith Johnstone (How To Books).

The Which? Guide To Changing Careers, Sue Bennett (Which? Books).

Planning Your Career in a Week, Wendy Hirsh and Charles Jackson (Hodder Education).

International

Getting A Job Abroad, Roger Jones (How To Books).

Headhunters

How To Be Headhunted, John Purkiss and Barbara Edlmair (How To Books).

Get Headhunted, Hilton Catt and Patricia Scudamore (Thompson Learning).

Consulting

The Successful Consultant, Susan Nash (How To Books).

Interviews and selection tests

Be Prepared! Getting Ready for Job Interviews, Julie-Ann Amos (How To Books).

Great Answers To Tough Interview Questions, Martin John Yate (Kogan Page), US.

Handling Tough Job Interviews, Julie-Ann Amos (How To Books).

How To Pass Selection Tests, Mike Bryon and Sanjay Modha (Kogan Page).

Passing That Interview, Judith Johnstone (How To Books).

Succeeding at Interviews, Judith Verity (How To Books).

Successful Interviews Every Time, Rob Yeung (How To Books).

The Perfect Answers to Interview Questions, Max Eggert (Arrow Business Books).

Useful Addresses

Career consultants

Career Analysts. www.careeranalysts.co.uk Tel: (020) 7935 5452.
Connaught Executive Ltd. www.connaughtexec.com Tel: 0800 980 0090.
Proteus Consultancy Limited, offices across the UK. www.proteus-net.co.uk Tel: 0870 760 6985.

General information

Recruitment and Employment Confederation. www.rec.uk.com Tel: (020) 7462 3260.

UK jobs online

Daily Telegraph, www.telegraph.co.uk
Financial Times, www.FT.com
www.monster.co.uk A huge range of vacancies, facility to post your CV and careers forums.
www.jobserve.com A relatively small site with a strong IT bias.
www.jobsite.co.uk A very good range of vacancies and some interesting career tools.
www.topjobs.co.uk A reasonable range of UK jobs.
www.totaljobs.co.uk A major recruitment site with careers advice, forums and salary checker.
www.workthing.com A smaller site than some of the others with a section on careers advice.

International jobs online

www.careerbuilder.com A great resource for jobs around the world. Links to a wide range of national sites including Europe, North America, Asia, the Far East and the Middle East.
www.careerone.com.au A major site for Australian jobs.
www.monster.com The parent of the UK site mentioned above and an excellent source for vacancies across Europe, North America, Asia and the Pacific Rim via a range of national sites.

Index